The Le

Paul West

For Marie-Claire,

You make me proud
that I know
you. Best regards
to you, with the
potent new book.

Paul

Onager Editions
Ithaca, New York

Onager Editions
PO Box 849
Ithaca, New York 14851-0849

The Left Hand is the Dreamer
by Paul West

Copyright © 2012 Paul West
ALL RIGHTS RESERVED

First Printing – December 2012
Cover artwork by Paul West
ISBN: 978-1-60047-807-9

This book is a work of non-fiction. All opinions expressed are solely those of the author and are not necessarily the views of Onager Editions.

No part of this book may be reproduced in any form, by photocopying or any electronic or mechanical means, including information storage or retrieval systems, without permission in writing from the copyright owner, except in the case of brief quotations embodied in critical articles and reviews.

Printed and bound in the United States of America

First Edition

5 4 3 2 1

The Left Hand is the Dreamer

by

Paul West

I dedicate this book, my fiftieth, to my beautiful, gifted wife and helpmate, Diane Ackerman, whose earlier book about my stroke was nominated for a Pulitzer Prize.

All three of my wonderful, caffeinated women, from Diane to Liz Butler and Melissa Townsend, saw me through that dark night of the soul called stroke and aphasia. May they continue to reign.

About Paul West

He now lives in Ithaca, New York. ("I'm a country boy, born and bred," he says, "I like trees and lawns, animals and huge silence.") West has been the recipient of numerous prizes and awards, including the Aga Khan Prize in 1974, a National Endowment for the Arts Fellowship in 1979 and 1985, the Hazlett Award for Excellence in the Arts in 1981, the Literature Award from the American Academy and Institute of Arts and Letters in 1985, a 1993 Lannan Prize for Fiction, and the Grand-Prix Halpèrine-Kaminsky for the Best Foreign Book in 1993. In 1994, the Graduate Schools of the Northeast gave West their Distinguished Teaching Award. He has also been named a Literary Lion by the New York Public Library and a Chevalier of the Order of Arts and Letters by the French Government. *The Tent of Orange Mist* was runner-up for the 1996 National Book Critics Circle Fiction Prize and the Nobel Prize for Literature. He's working on his fiftieth book.

BOOKS BY PAUL WEST

FICTION

The Shadow Factory
The Immensity of the Here and Now
Cheops
A Fifth of November
O.K.
The Dry Danube
Life with Swan
Terrestrials
Sporting with Amaryllis
The Tent of Orange Mist
Love's Mansion
The Women of Whitechapel and Jack the Ripper
Lord Byron's Doctor
The Place in Flowers Where Pollen Rests
The Universe, and Other Fictions
Rat Man of Paris
The Very Rich Hours of Count von Stauffenberg
Gala
Colonel Mint
Caliban's Filibuster
Bela Lugosi's White Christmas
I'm Expecting to Live Quite Soon
Alley Jaggers
Tenement of Clay
Now, Voyager

NONFICTION

My Father's War
Tea with Osiris
Oxford Days
Master Class
New Portable People
The Secret Lives of Words
My Mother's Music
A Stroke of Genius
Sheer Fiction-Volumes I, II, III, IV
Portable People
Out of My Depths: A Swimmer in the Universe
Words for a Deaf Daughter
I, Said the Sparrow
The Wine of Absurdity
The Snow Leopard
The Modern Novel
Byron and the Spoiler's Art
James Ensor

CHAPTERS

1. The Fatal Swoon
2. Intensive Care
3. A Diffident Double-Tap
4. Niele
5. Francis
6. Not Gruesome At All
7. Kim
8. In Amazement
9. Carmen and Patricia
10. "My Momma Died"
11. Manifest
12. Apraxia
13. Rigor and Zeal
14. Some Penitent Angel
15. The Physiatrist
16. No Life at the Equator
17. Jessica and Sayeed
18. One Trick
19. Anti-Spasticity
20. We'll Walk
21. In a Bauhaus Sort of Way
22. Underground Man
23. Trysts
24. Bemused As I Often Am
25. Among the Valiant
26. Calendar
27. Came the Day
28. Rialto
29. Landscape
30. 220 Pounds
31. Labor Day, 2011
32. Trying to Tell a Story
33. Self-Similar
34. Beyond Everything

1

The Fatal Swoon

I fell, came crashing down. Injuring my leg, immobilizing my right arm and paralyzing my right cheek. Not so much an accident as an insult to half my body, which after a few days of elementary care turned into a full blown stroke, leaving me mumbling, unable to speak.

Look at him, Diane whispered, *he's having another stroke.* One glance at my dreadful pallor sufficed—coupled with my frozen eyes and expressionless face. In what seemed like no time at all, I was flat on my back beneath a colossal lamp hearing Diane speak with the doctor about my condition.

What caused this idiot to go full tilt, stumbling catastrophically when merely crossing my living room in pursuit of a book titled *Therapies*? Feeling for the book's exaggerated title? Just possibly, but I doubt it. More likely a mere instant of mental vacancy leading to unstable footing. The millisecond for all time.

To have taken the plunge from one dimension to another may seem upward gesture, a gesture of joy. But not so. For me it was rather a fatal swoon towards oblivion.

2

Intensive Care

In the confines of Intensive Care, I endured the first of what I have learned to call out-of-body experiences. I was wholly enclosed in a metallic room. When the door opened, I was grabbed by an officious looking gent in horn-rimmed glasses and a female nurse, whom I felt I faintly recognized. Without more ado the gent divested me of my rags and pronounced me "Fit to be tried."

I thought I heard him say: "He has the beginning of a fistula, and is not too clean, but he'll pass for the time being. Fit subject for the French." Without more ado, they hoisted me up to heaven to wait and watch the latest offering, the Children of the Reich. Of the familiar nurse I could see no sign.

The neurologist on teleconference advised Diane to give me an anti-clotting agent, Tissue Plasminogen Activator, also known as TPA. I remember Diane's reply, "He has had one stroke already. It might kill him."

"He might be better off. Think on that."

Diane decided against TPA, and it was fortunate for me.

Admitted to the hospital, I fell again, dropped to the floor by two male handlers. I was too heavy. Any type of excuse. Rather, they did not have their minds on their jobs, dreaming of being blown by the wide-mouthed nurses, having nothing intellectually better to do. I was a mute, a runaway toy to them, right arm and leg paralyzed, portent for disaster and not worth caring about. The result was my first migraine in years. My head buzzed and spun as I strove to master the whirlwind within my skull. Fat chance.

This was real. So was my next adventure, a surprise evacuation, relocation to a luxury suite on the top hospital floor, a hospital wing with a reputation for neckties. My new accommodations were a gift from a well-wisher with an appetite for my books; my room adjoined a cocktail lounge of lavish display with champagne and Burmese silks, akin to places sumptuous like Shangri-La.

My tongue felt thick, unwieldy, and uncontrollable. Speaking was impossible and more dangerously, I could not swallow. I could not eat or drink. There were doctors—I called them Quislings—even in that paradise of medical learning, suggesting surgical intervention as a fitting way out for a fellow like me. I was at risk for this plot, but for my protector, a Harvard medical man who would not let the Quislings implant a darkly rumored feeding tube in my abdomen to stave off my declining calorie count. He held them off, these Quislings, until they finally lost interest in me and sought other creatures to pillage.

Meanwhile, the bush telegraph of my upstairs Valhalla announced in its fickle way the imminent presence of a visitor from of all places, my native England. This worthy personage turned out to be an admirer of mine from Manchester. He asked about Diane, in whose praises he was unstinting. I perked up, marveling at his bluff Manchester accent and the breadth of his reading. It was a heavenly respite.

3

A Diffident Double-Tap

Came the final day of my residence on hospital's cloud nine, with its roomy accommodations, impeccable staff, and view smothered in palm trees. I was destined for Rehabilitation, for how long God alone knew.

After hoisting me aloft on a stretcher, the driver whisked me along the freeway to my next abode, fifty miles away among Florida's convalescent homes, there to mend my ailing system or break in the attempt.

We were directed to a certain room, 309, with two uncomfortable looking twin beds and a perfunctory bathroom. A diffident double tap broke the silence of the door, announcing a flaxen haired young woman with an authoritarian manner who introduced herself as a therapist. She had a trumpeting voice reared in France and a dazzling, sun-coming-out smile that made you forgive the voice. "I'm here to see how well you manage your shirt."

"Ahhh." I garbled.

"Manage your shirt."

"Uhhhhh."

"I mean put it on."

There ensued a paradox of motion, with me, one-handed, trying to put on a clean shirt that resisted all help and ended in a straggly heap of clothes at my feet with obvious results. A man with his right hand useless is an untidy spectacle worthy of the best comedians.

In a trice she showed me how to do it. And again and again until I was proficient at least to shirt wranglers of the old school.

"Got it?" She asked steadily, there was a politeness in her brazen voice.

"Urr…."

She repeated her name, whisked away out the door, and left me agape. I had been among the shirtless ones, now alas reprieved.

I was like an elephant who, to his surprise, is reduced to finding among the hoi polloi of human species a kindred call, still further reduced to crying aphonetically aloud for his human shirt, minus one leg, one arm.

All this and I was in a wheelchair!

My first night I spent in penitential discontent, the bed's air mattress inflating and deflating every five minutes or so, the consequence of a pneumatic device ordered by the doctors to resist the bedsores I was afflicted with. I woke, presuming I had slept at all, hearing the sound of a puppy being eviscerated in awful agony, it seemed.

"Put that dog out of his misery," I shouted in an incomprehensible slur above the clang of the preparation of breakfast. Still the tumult went on, reaching now and then a high pitch which subsided into a kind of slobbering as the poor animal paused for breath.

I was wrong. The sound I'd heard was that of the breakfast trolley advancing, making a hysterical crescendo as it lumbered forward, dispensing fried eggs for some, oatmeal for others. The sounds I had heard were echoes of my oversensitive brain pushed too far by the sleepless night full of the sighings of my strange heaving bed.

Why no one thought to fix the wheel of the cart, I shall never know. The forlorn, love-starved cry will occupy my thoughts to the end of my days.

Speaking of Hell, I remember what the doctor had said regarding my aching shoulder, *sublux*, which I took to mean when something, say a bone, had fallen from its rightful place. Gradually the word in my mind has taken on a sexual meaning, obscene and random, but visibly a penis, to add a stiff burden of complexity to its former concept.

    The structure of morning was becoming clear. Rude awaking at 8:00 o'clock, after an untidy night insulted by a shower of my own piss on my bed due to the aide whose assistance with a urinal was askew. Followed by breakfast and shower. First glimpse of the enemy at 9:30, who happened to be an inappropriately pretty black haired saint, the speech therapist Kim Vaughn.

    Kim soon had me practicing vowel sounds, especially "o" and "a," while she launched into a discussion of politics, of which I was an amateur by choice. My brain was not in the least cloudy, but the sounds I made were. Pure apraxia. I had lost control of my mouth. My lips, my tongue, even my cheeks felt frozen, sloppy, would not obey. I was indeed a poor slob.

    What did Kim say to me before taking her leave? "Floor above you is where we keep the hopeless. Keep them until they die. You are one of the fortunate ones." She was right. Despite as disconsolate as I felt, being unable to speak, arm dangling by my side, with my useless leg. Kim delivered me to my next destination and we entered the huge cavernous rehabilitation room that became my home away from home.

Blind eyes turned in greeting—I saw limp limbs worn with grace and manifest pride. Some patients even tokened a salute to me, the newcomer. Overweight ladies, the talkers of this town as well as a few gaunt and stranded-looking men, habitués of death's door. A motley crew to be sure, but for whom visual originality was an art form, composed of the wasted, the malformed, the deprived, the damned. One could live an eternity in such a place without running out of cannon fodder. Or to put in another way, without denial of the human condition by the lord of hosts in a bad mood.

I knew at that moment I would write about them all. With my right (writing) hand frozen, all to be written by my left hand. To be soon written on the wind. Left alone, surveying my fate, I viewed myself as one who having run his course, runs amok, content to savor life whenever possible.

4
Niele

Niele, patroness of the practicum of putting on my shirt, interrupted my vengeful reverie to ask if I prefer hot or cold towels.

"Warhhh." I responded as if taking a photograph of my own voice denatured by stress and strain, barely noise at all.

"What?" demanded my female inquisitor as if questioning a fox.

I made answer in my best pidgin. "All ooyar."

"On what?" amazed.

"Ooyar."

She saw at last the extent of my handicap, but allowed license.

"Waarhhmm."

"Warm. I'll be back soon."

Niele deserted, no mention of a tussle with a shirt, leaving me to take stock of my surroundings. On my left I viewed a young woman, one eye fixed unwinkingly on me, the other fixed on some unknown star, perhaps Algol. On my right was a woman, at least three hundred pounds, who talked incessantly. I wondered if she talked in her sleep. It took several people to lift her upright to her feet from her chair, she talking all the time to her lifters who pretended not to notice her prattle. She was a permanent resident who would never get out.

On her return, Niele massaged my shoulders. Her manner during all this was grand; my body relaxed, muscles softer than before. And for the first time I thought that all could be well with me and my condition. Such is the power of faith and healing touch.

After massaging my shoulder and arm and hand, she continued her task, stretching and flexing the muscles and joints, sometimes painfully while asking incessantly "Does it hurt?" My answer was always in the negative. After ten seconds of treatment, I was exhausted and begged for reprieve, but was only allowed after ten minutes more.

A cultural hybrid, she was as if her French body had fused with her English, both sides of her lineage coming together in stately harmony. I was certain she even played cricket with a French accent. My massage done, she tended to someone else, but not before she renewed my faith with the majestic facial aubade she had probably learned in school.

As I would come to know well, with her knowing hands Niele distributed her wares equally between oafs and caballeros. She would set my right hand in motion again after a long month of complete quiescence. Niele never troubled again me about my shirt, though she tested many others.

For now, the frozen fingers of my right hand refused to budge, despite all my efforts. "A hand with a will of its own," Niele judged. She had tried again and again to free it of its iron clamp, but the answer was no. *Non servinam*, I blithely attempted to pronounce to deify the occasion, which Niele took in her stride as French. We left it be, at least until tomorrow at the same time, same place. "Time for Francis to have you," she merrily went on her way to coffee, leaving a pell-mell of goodwill behind. Niele was mistress of a good deal more than shirts.

5

Francis

Time 10:30. A moment of respite in which I was free to meditate on my condition. I was not yet ready to perform humble human magic tricks such as walking upright without stumbling, or surviving Niele's ceremonial hot towels without gasping for life. In ten minutes or so I would meet Francis, the physical therapist of the multi-talented group assembled here to rehabilitate in the main gymnasium.

I had noticed Francis already, his inimitable saunter through the crowd, his quick black eyes, frequent yelps of triumph and his deft twists and turns of patients ambulating off-course, to prevent certain collision. He was a rather small man, but a power in the land. I was prepared to know him and his tribe of acolytes to my infinite improvement. Francis had the answer to everything physical and the cure as well, to use the French for a moment, *se conduire*. He knew what he was driving.

I noticed, as time dragged on with no appearance from Sir Francis, that patients having wheelchairs developed a superior countenance, an air as if committed to the grand life. While those whose destiny was in doubt were entitled to much better beds in which to breathe their last. The latter people caught my eye as they swept past on their final journey, or neared it—they seemed to be winking or crooking a finger at me, wishing me a pleasant flight into the hereafter. Not gruesome at all, not superior.

At last, Francis appeared. Nothing befits a man more than enjoying a very high office and making love to it on every visible opportunity, especially with women to watch. Francis was much more humble than that, except for lapsing into an exaggerated swagger of his hips. In truth, he was a modest man with extraordinary technical skill, and an enormous sagacity when confronted with the thousand and one challenges that arise during the daily affairs of any institution such as The Gardens Court skilled nursing center.

I once saw Francis leap seven feet, gaining momentum as he passed, airborne, from one box to another. Not to be outdone, he repeated the feat, to much applause. First time, wonderment. Second time, cheering. Within my time span in his company, he was never known to repeat the *tour de force*. One could see why. On the other hand, why not? He left us guessing. Perhaps he has already performed it. Perhaps not. At any rate, Francis merits kudos for many things, not least teaching one recusant how to exercise.

Without more ado, Francis requested I show my paces, poor that they were. He noted weak calves and weaker thighs, not much endurance and poor wind. One lame leg and one lame arm. I was a specimen to be reckoned with as all could see.

Francis looked me up and down and I immediately hatched a plan of self survival.

He queried, "What have you been doing to yourself?"

"I fell." I slurred.

He studied me with a palpable concern. "Age?"

"81." A blurt.

"That's nothing to us." A monastic pause. "First, try our recumbent bike, just to get warmed up."

With his help, I clambered upon the framework and he secured my feet on the pedals, which felt remarkably easy to spin. At once he adjusted them to make the spin more difficult, announcing with a wink, "We don't want you to believe we are a race of mini-pandas, do we? Ok. Cycle for a quarter of an hour please. And no cheating."

"Not me." I stammered.

"Oh, I've seen all types of men come here and lie to us."

I cycled. My strong leg pedaled and my weak one slept while it spun its circles. Francis and I were off on an unlikely escapade, and I could envision the results of this first magical ride infinitely improving into the distance.

Here was Francis, an amateur golfer and a high-class performer of high jinks for select audiences, with his daughter in the process of making up her mind whether she would attend Harvard, just one of several prestigious options. And now Francis had taken on a writer with a disobedient imagination. My first physical task was not to let him down, come what may.

Twelve chimed on the rococo clock above our heads. Lunchtime, a festival honored by all—the legless, the armless, the brainless, and even those without words. Classes would resume at 1:30 pm for those eager to begin again. Someone wheeled me back to my room, back to my bed and the urine stained sheets. I wondered in my meandering way why American women did not know how to properly make a bed, with the bottom sheets tucked in, lest half-way through the night you'd be embroiled in a mess of impossible to retrieve blankets. What further perversions would grace this scene, I could not know, but they would be something bestial and complete.

6

Not Gruesome At All

Long ago, as a boy in England, I dreamed of the USA as a place to travel to, all swing music and ice-cream, Duke Ellington jazz, the lesser lights such as Benny Carter, and the different flavors of peppermint and horehound sweets. But that in a previous century. I mordantly expected my lunch to be a horrid vision, perhaps roach fricassee, steamed skunk droppings on the side, but found a plateful of roast chicken and lasagna followed by cream puff and ice cream. Thank God I was now able to swallow. One bite at a time, rest 30 seconds, then another bite. It was exhausting work, but I was ravenous. Dinner to follow would be another enviable feast.

Roast chicken cures the mind of most ill-thoughts, especially those of an 81-year old cynic. So it was with abstract delight that I waited like a panting dog for lunch and dinner the whole of my three month stay at Gardens Court. Culinary bliss was every day, and not just my breakfast of twinned poached eggs and sausage triplets.

After lunch, I slept the sleep of the just for three hours, awaking feeling uncommonly refreshed, but not up for afternoon calisthenics. After heaven-sent sumptuous dinner, the evening would be devoted to the intelligentsia, Rachel Maddow, who had attended Lincoln College, Oxford, as had I, several years earlier. Never let it be said that my patriotic zeal was wanting. By and large, Maddow was the only political commentator I could stand, with the exception of Ed Schultz of the Ed Show whose evening program I relished but only made it through the first half-hour, when sleep again called, which I ensured by taking a half-pill of Ativan. Life was shaping up a new routine in several ways.

Dyna, the arch-priest of the spilled urine—three such spills before she quit in disgrace—was replaced by Liz, a treasured friend who had spent seven years as my literary assistant. Liz made sense of the shower of pharmaceuticals that had descended on me and among her abundant gifts there was the knack of dealing with paperwork, hysteria, and placating officials. Liz was a fully-trained Registered Nurse, who charmed the staff of the rehab units with her rapid talk and her book-a-day reading habit. How she had room for all this and a home life eludes, but she did. To this recitation of her excellence—Did I mention she is also the dynamite speller who recently compiled the 1101 pages of the manuscript I had been diligently working on—until I had my catastrophic fall?

7
Kim

Kim began each speech session by enjoining me to whistle, which is to say use an instrument through which I blew out and then inhaled. This practice, she explained, can expand your lungs by half as much again. Honestly. I believed. I blew. I inhaled. And the results would prove her point.

Then Kim once again spouted off on another subject entirely, this time her cherished hobby of jewelry-making at which she had won several prizes. I was amazed to find a first class medical professional so talented in a second skill.

She obliged when asked to provide therapy upstairs among the lost. She accepted willingly, but with *amour propre* at being torn from her primary work to this vocation among the fatal. The carrying of so much responsibility should have made her into a testy automaton, but not a bit of it, her demeanor remained personable, benign, charismatic throughout.

Kim moved on to discuss techniques to engage my mouth, opening it to pronounce, *Kah, Pah,* and *Tah*. And solemnly repeat *Coke, Cook, Cake,* and vigorously, *K-ing, K-ong*. I did as I was told, recollecting old-style British methods of recitation in my classes in Eckington primary school.

I was also to obey her injunction to pucker my lips, to puff out my cheeks, stick out my tongue, and to push the tip of my tongue back and forth into each cheek. The remedy for all things was to say *pah*, *tah*, and *kah* slowly six times each. Then I would get to the promised land of intelligible speech. But not yet. Now was Kim's strict academy, mine own private boot camp fresh from hell. Results not yet ready for public consumption.

At last, Kim delivered me again to Niele, who had warm compresses ready to apply before we played with rehabilitative toys—plastic cones, fuzzy dice, washcloths, and such other niceties.

I had overheard Niele described in various ways, not all of them polite, with local prejudice, but you had to know Niele first to appreciate the sunny, fun-loving part of her disposition, the way she rationed sunlight, answering questions with an interrogative, tossing out the challenge implicit in the matter of the shirt, for instance.

Always after Niele, back to the man I soon called Francis the Compassionate Slavedriver. Francis with his faultless English, whether the subject was highly technical or simple as ABC. Educated in the Philippines, he must have been well instructed by his tutors, it was as if Francis knew it all from the first.

His philosophy was simple. Go for the extra yard. He lived to teach, always pushing his pupils, as he had been pushed, and I can tell you firsthand, they always respond. Despite the pain, we gave back in kind.

The twenty-odd rehab folk became accustomed to my unshaven face, omnipresent polo shirt, and habit of wearing golf shorts indoors in obeisance to the Florida sun. A few lucky people walked abroad among us, freed from their shackles and chairs. Envious looks accompanied them as they sported their newfound freedom. No apology uttered as they crossed over the threshold for the last time, no lingering glance at the crew they left behind. On to their winding-sheets and final strut. This was the world I attempted to regain.

8

In Amazement

I was spavined from this second day's calisthenics. I wanted sleep and lunch in that order. Once again, sleep for three hours, lunch at three pm followed by dinner at five. A hodge-podge of a renegade schedule.

I was awakened by the sound of more diffident knocking. Lucian, a Spaniard, wanted to bestow another local ritual—to weigh me. Off we wheeled down the hallways, eager to weigh and be weighed. The verdict? 195 pounds. "Better cut back your appetite," said Lucian, "or they'll do it for you."

This second night passed in the blur of fatigue. I was unfortunately roused from fitful sleep at 5:15 am by an official in search of my blood for his lab. Blinded by his lamp, I offered my veins for the specimen without comment. I spent the next two hours miserably awake in contemplation of my navel and my withered right hand; bending it back and forth with my left to facilitate the passage of blood flow. This was the technique used by Comrade Niele herself.

Wake at 8 am, wash and brush up, breakfast at 8:30, wheeled down to meet Kim for 9:30, then Niele at 11:00 plus Francis at 12. More or less my daily timetable, followed by lunch, three hours of sleep, then dinner shortly to follow.

I look back in amazement at how rapidly I adapted to living this day in, day out. I, the circadian-defying night owl, accustomed to rising at noon, staying up all night, and going to bed at 5 am. I must have been waiting all my life for something like this to happen, something so formulaic and exact, defying my chronological will. It dared come true.

Call it regimentation. The daily schedule and communal quarters reminded me of the three years I'd spent in the Royal Air Force. But in the Air Force there was cricket to be had, and social life in the evening with the local lasses. Here the inmates brought broken bodies, desperate for a fix to while away their remaining time, with dreams of prowess achieved, and gone alas too soon. They remained cheerful, buoyant almost, but always with the wheelchair at the dream end.

I had been relegated to the category of *aspiring*, caught in the dance of caregivers. Some to fail before others, but en masse doomed to hear the last trumpet sounding for them. No wonder we responded to the tonic appeal of calisthenics, the last bridge to nowhere. Others had made it out, so why not I?

Here I pause to amplify my loss of speech. How such a creature as myself, the author of 50 books, can settle for communication so primitive when all the time the mind within is trying to escape its injured bonds. Demeaned to first strive vainly for crude expression of *A, B, C*, then the thrill of progress from that ship of fools to the next best thing, the proto-language of *Hi, Just Fine, Howdy*.

When speech fails and no one understands what you have to say, all that is left to the enterprising soul is the language of sullen shrugs or the keyhole formed by two fingers entwined together, signifying *I'm OK*. The only language left for me the language of the mute; the language of true men left unspoken among the speechless hell of this prison. But thousands have got by with less, and thousands more will succeed them.

No wonder I became known as the silent man of the whole pastiche. With so few people silent, I hoarded my words against my final demise. But I was respected for being a sobersides, my paltry *Hi's* and *Fine* doing duty for reams of backchat. At present I was a silent man, but a silent man who knew the score.

9
Carmen and Patricia

Things began to assemble into their proper places. Liz did the morning shift, winning hearts and minds with her sensibility and steady repartee. She took weekends off, turning up each of her five days as I churned from Kim, to Niele, to Francis.

We hired Carmen from a private agency to watch over me on evenings and weekends. Carmen was a different cat entirely; in her soft-spoken way she was blissfully in charge of things and would not be gainsaid. I still can hear her patent leather voice cajoling me to be silent while I submitted myself to her rituals. "Must put the ointment on first. There, that's the groin. Roll over please. Thank you, Mr. West. Wonderful. Now I prepare to wipe your bum. God knows what lurks there. And, that's better, isn't it?"

This on for a full ten minutes culminating in assistance with a shower or a complete inspection of my problem areas—armpits, teeth, and molars. I imagined, "Next, Mr. West, will be your brain."

At home, next task for Carmen was Russian, which she was learning from a friend. And games of tennis against her husband, whom she revered with passionate good nature. Her daughter had dreams of becoming a psychiatrist, aiming at Cornell or some similarly illustrious school—the daughter already a tennis ace, with nowhere to go but up. Indeed they were a tennis family, and I could envision their dining room plastered with trophies. Carmen was a riot, gentle and original and enough of a malaprop to make style-worthy.

With Liz and Carmen to guide my comings and goings within the giant rehab machine, what could go wrong?

Beyond the din made, mainly at breakfast-time, by the cleaning staff, the scullery maids, the brute workforce of those who hung onto a paltry job instead of being unemployed. (This I approved of, being an ex-unemployed myself.) At the tops of their lungs, the incessant chorus of over-stressed voices, all committed to making the biggest uproar since Christ freed the slaves of Babylon.

Some kind soul had equipped me with a packet of plush purple earplugs to withstand the blast of the neighbor's TV, so I employed them to deaden out the cacophony. A successful stratagem, I'm pleased to say. The barrage continued at a lower decibel, as if muted in some simulacrum of abolished sound. I felt reprieved, fortified by the set of plugs, however diminished they made the world sound, faintly like a squirrel scratching or a politician scratching his hair. I returned to the mental privacy of my wheelchair, happily muffled in the interests of peace.

The staff did not last long, but were replaced every few weeks by compatriots of equal timber. Perhaps they went to people denuded waxworks or to shore up a political party distinguished by noise.

There was more to come, in the form of a plague of mosquitos which feasted on me while I was sleeping, and then attended to Carmen, sleeping in the equally infested bunk next to mine. We disposed of them but the buzzing, pestilent memory was not easy to banish.

The next morning, after putting me through my paces in the mildest possible way (mistaking my pronunciation of *theme* for tame and *weight* for height), Kim handed me off to Niele, who requested I trace a sweeping motion with my weak hand on a tabletop. To be performed while standing up.

Forward and back, forward and back. After ten minutes of this, I lost my balance, collapsing to the ground, legs crossed in a heap as a cry welled up of "Man down, man down!" It took five people to help me back to my feet with the assistance of a capacious sheet whose texture I remember as bosomy, enveloping, of the earth earthy. I felt fine.

Why so uninjured? Perhaps because, taught by Francis, I had learned to fall. A series of gradual steps was the key to going down gracefully. Precise words for so inviolate and ungraceful an art. At any rate, I fell again, this time as if my life did not depend on it.

Expressions of relief and disbelief abounded among the staff, particularly the incredulous repetition of, "Only the second fall in Niele's 16 years on the job."

I was getting famous at last.

I had faith nothing serious had taken place, but it might have. A few healed scratches would make me whole again. It could have ended differently. A break to my weakened leg could have put me on quieter street forever. Things seemed to be looking up, an emotion I fall prey to, I felt a surge of fellow feeling—life was better than it seemed, compared to only yesterday.

Could it truly be that I was settling in after all? After all the strife of moving into yet another place, the good ship of my discontented soul had landed upstream among civilized, sane people? It was hard to believe.

Wait a moment, though. I must rein in my goodwill. There are exceptions, surely, from maladroit shirts to the breakfast whinny of the molested dog, from mosquitos of the night to the 5 am invasion of the blood sucker from the lab.

And why does a bevy of people—nurses, social workers, aides, doctors—wait until *lunch* when my mouth is chock full of delights before besieging me with questions? It makes me gulp. And my mouth splutter.

There must be more to this roll call of amateur devils. Perhaps I was becoming reasonable in my old age, forgiving and mellow. I demurred to pursue, letting the other villains slip by.

Life was now in short supply. The difference between 80 and 81 is tremendous. You live five years in the interim, then anticipation reveals they have already passed, never to return. And the keenest joys you were ever to know have receded into what John Keats—who knew about these things—called the spirit ditties of no tone.

Keats knew all right, even though his own allotment of days was very short. Yet, in fact, the difference between his short-lived days and mine was similar, as is usually about such things as life and death. That phrase of his, *the spirit ditties of no tone*, signals us to watch out. The worst has already happened and we must (*I* must) go on with the consequences as best we may.

To lighten the load on Liz and Carmen, we found Patricia, a fabulous talker and another book-a-day reader, divorced, Russian and Red Indian. Patricia, it was felt by the Sanhedrin (Liz and Kim and Carmen), would persuade me to talk more and sensibly. Patricia was a jet-black haired woman with a regal manner, tough, literate and an ambivalent hater of clocks (read what follows). Punctilious to a fault and a believer in etiquette, she had my books.

One evening, soon after Patricia arrived, she vented her usual tirade to noisome clocks, maintaining the tick was driving her batty. Liz decided to remedy, replacing the offensive timepiece with an identical twin, silent as the grave. When Patricia next arrived at 7 pm for an evening stint, she complained she could no longer hear the tick, which she declaimed as her mainstay.

My next marvel was the young nurses who staffed the Gardens Court. They confronted me wherever I looked. The girls talked nonstop, mainly about boyfriends, but occasionally wandering off subject to report medical emergencies or, in hushed voices, near misses of pregnancy or the effect of husband's missives to Viagra.

All giving the inmates something to get excited about. Otherwise, one whiled away the hours waiting for the ladies among the inmates to roll up in their wheelchairs, especially those with eyes to see or with legs to flourish. The men with truly bad strokes lay back in their wheelchairs and scanned the caverns of their minds for memories of depravities long gone, their peeling open the first pair of knickers and of getting a faint whiff of rubber mingled with silky asafetida.

Still adjusting to life as a one-handed man. I found myself in a predicament. Imagine yourself into this: a bag of potato chips with your only working hand unable to withdraw itself! Always I had hope for better than this; my good hand held captive while holding onto something salty and tangy, prevented from ending in a final salubrious chomp.

My working hand was imprisoned in the glossy plastic bag with no chance of escape, while my bag-holding hand was defunct and could not assist. And thus I remained stuck until I tipped the bag to my mouth and ate—hand still inside—until I was able to free myself to eat another bag of chips.

No matter how I felt about my own status, condition, predicament (whatever you may choose to call it), there were some things I could rely upon—Liz and Patricia and especially Carmen. The first two could be counted upon to give me a wash and brush-up, just missing out on the beastliest things, but Carmen flung caution to the wind and washed penis and groin and especially well the rear end, pulling from nowhere a series of buttered cloths, inspiring her commentary, "Soiled yourself, and properly today," or

"Dry today. What have you done to ensure such result?"

All I had to do is bare my bum backward. I was struck with amazement at such a turn. I wondered how this show had come about? It took courage for Carmen to do this while remaining debonair, chattering all those lighthearted things while pulling the pudding of an elephant—as I still sometimes thought of myself.

Aghast, I wondered at the female venturesome spirit that takes them into the unknown region to seek what they can find. Rumble thy bellyful, says King Lear in one of his accurate moments.

10

"My Momma Died"

Samantha Williams, scullery maid mainly present at breakfast and lunch, arrived with a proposition. She was buxom, wordy, and broke. "My momma died this Thursday and I will fly to Jamaica for her burial. Any help would be welcome." Patricia and I stared at Samantha's unbecoming countenance encrusted with the remains of her breakfast of damsons and poached egg. Panhandling was forbidden at Gardens Court. We shooed her away with sympathetic reluctance.

By week's end, Samantha was the worse for wear, with the same story about Momma. Carmen and I dispatched her with minimal courtesy. This was Samantha's last appeal, and we wondered if she was in her right mind, or haunted by some childhood tragedy or baroque Jamaican racial memory. She went to the funeral and we never saw her again—banished by an over-scrupulous supervisor or engulfed in the memory of her mother, to whose last act she had been invited?

To add to woes, the cap of my front tooth had broken, leaving me gap-toothed, snaggly, and in need of repair. Liz and I made haste to the dentist's office, not so much an office as a space made over for dentistry and storage. We gained access to the room via the dreaded upper floor, running the gauntlet of the truly decrepit waiting to die. Past the aid station with no hope, the dentist was located in an out-of-use shower stall capable of being commandeered for the purposes of the living (and the dead).

Frankly bewildered, we plunged in the door to be met by a grandiose dentist with a stammer, heavily veined arms, and a mammoth gold ring. Taking a suspiciously unsanitary tube of what looked like glue from his gym bag, he mixed the cement, tapping my tooth back into place, all the while whistling music off-key between his false teeth which did not fit. "Bite down hard then wait twenty minutes before lunch. And try not to come back." My pleasure.

11

Manifest

Meanwhile a complete manifest of my medications magically appeared, tamed in typeface on a crisp sheet of paper. The list's typical hand-scrawled, globular appearance made inspiringly legible. Which is the more palatable version, I wondered, as the barely decipherable schedule made its first readable appearance. My life depended on the lucidity of the regimen, it's true, but it seemed to me its curvier hand-penned embodiment had been more human. This new version, with columnar stature, appeared more machine, more amenable into a death sentence. Of course, either visage could be lethal, given incompetence or evil intent, but I am assessing two-dimensional appearances only. I was glad to have a schedule by me, nonetheless, even though the thrice a day medication routine, with bilious taste and cough-inducing aspirations was no great enjoyable mouthful.

    My daily ration of pills, without which my chances were hopeless, was as medical management goes, not a bad bargain—cheap at the price and visually stimulating to boot. I could manage without these pink and green and white tablets with their entertaining shapes, but not for long. Medication, with its life-enhancing tendency, is a boon to nature and therefore should not be pillorized lightly, routine and mindless as it has become in the hands of this drug-dependent generation. What we would be without medicines? A poorer, more timid human, not so long for this earth, and closer to the cherished animals.

MEDICATION	
PRESCRIPTION	
allopurinol 3 x 100 mg pills 300 mg	1x/day
Coreg (carvedilol) 12.5mg	2x/day
Coumadin (DAW) 4 mg/1mg (dose per PT results)	1x/day
Diovan (DAW) 160 mg	1x/day
Glucophage (metformin HCl) 500 mg (1000mg am, 1000mg pm) ORDER from TEVA or SANDOZ	2 tablets 2x/day
Lipitor (DAW) 20 mg	1x/day
Precose (acarbose) 100 mg	3x/day
Zoloft (sertraline HCL) 50 mg	1x/day
OTC	
OTC-Aspirin 81 mg	1x/day
OTC Multi-vitamin	1x/day
OTC Iron Supplement Ferrous Sulfate 65 mg (Feosol)	1x/day
PRN	
Astelin Nasal Spray (137 mcg) (azelastine HCl) For nasal congestion 2 sprays each nostril 2x/day (am and pm)	
Maxair autoinhaler (pirbuterol acetate inhalation aerosol) For respiratory congestion 2 puffs every am and/or For shortness of breath (no more than 2 puffs every four hours)	
PRN (as needed) 2 Liters O2 by nasal cannula at night	

MUST eat food before taking meds

MUST be out of bed to eat breakfast (OK to sit upright with pillows behind back to have some milk if you're waiting for someone to help transfer out of bed).

Splint

Right arm/hand at all times. May take breaks. To prevent contracture. Remind him that it's the way to save his writing hand—so it doesn't get stuck from contracture while PT works on regaining use of his fingers.

Shaving

Encourage. Physical Therapist says the external stimulation is good for his cheek/throat muscles.

Most Frequent Requests

He likes to have Kleenex available within reach of his L hand

Milk

Safety Risks/Mobility

Recliner is electric. The button to move recliner is by Paul's right arm. ESSENTIAL to UNPLUG recliner when Paul is sitting in the chair, as his right elbow can drop, hit button, and cause chair to tip him forwards/backwards!

Two person transfer. Strong pivot on L leg. R leg still weak, occasionally buckles. Verbal cues helpful.

Physical therapist or very experienced aide can do one person transfer. There have been problems with transferring Paul—it's worth asking the aide/nurse if they've moved him before.

Commode

Orthostatic hypotension. Paul's had a few episodes. Be careful during transfers. If he complains of dizziness, not feeling right—take blood pressure. If low—back to bed, feet elevated, head down. Paul's BP meds were adjusted (dose decreased) Sunday March 13.

Swallowing/Food/Liquid

Much Improved.

Per Kim, Speech Therapist:

PAUL MAY HAVE SMALL PIECES OF ICE CHIPS. One at a time, throughout the day.

MUST be sitting upright at 90 degrees, or sitting forward. In chair is best, pillows behind back or sitting forward to maintain position.

Paul can eat without coughing/aspirating, ONLY if he is in the correct position.

Chin tuck. Paul can self-monitor this. Remind as necessary.

DO NOT LET HIM EAT/DRINK while watching TV. (He looks up towards the TV/aspirates).

Feeds himself with left hand.

Nectar thick liquids. Pureed solids (often foods are too thick, add hot water or gravy to reach puree consistency).

Cover Paul with hospital gown as napkin (it's a messy process!)

Paul will often ask for milk throughout the day. There are boxes of nectar-thick milk in and on top of fridge. He's been using the small blue plastic cups.

Output

We are no longer keeping track of I and O. His fluid intake is fine.

He will ask for commode/urinal, but may not be clear, so if he's asking for something and you can't tell what he's saying, point to the urinal/commode. May say "peepee" for urinal. Usually uses soon upon waking.

Equipment

Commode.

The basin receptacle needs to be positioned correctly (NO GAPS). It's easy to put back the wrong way, which causes urine to go all over the floor. Worth double-checking!

Climate

Air conditioner control/thermostat is in far left (no handle) closet. Paul usually likes it a little warm (air con off at night)—ask if he wants on for afternoon nap if room is hot.

Medications

Administered by Gardens Court Staff.

CRUSHED only in pudding/applesauce.

Paul will want to have milk available to help wash them down.

Nystatin Powder mixed with Baza antifungal (mix in palm) to groin 2 x/day.
Wash area gently, and dry thoroughly before application
Important, this area is becoming more irritated.

MED SCHEDULE
9 am meds
Coreg 12.5 mg
Precose 100 mg
Iron supplement
aspirin 81 mg x/2

5pm
Diovan 160 mg

9 pm meds
Lantus Insulin
Zoloft 50 mg 1x/day
Lipitor 20 mg 1x/day

Allopurinol 300 mg 1x/day

Coumadin as directed

Precose 100 mg

Coreg 12.5 mg

10pm-ish

Ativan, prn, for sleep

Respiratory Congestion

Paul may have prn every 6 hours

Xopenex/Levalbuterol HCL .63mg nebulizer treatment

Sitting him upright will help him cough effectively

Sleep

At night he may ask for/you may offer Ativan (sleeping medication) around 10 pm—or later in the night if he is restless.

2 L Oxygen by nasal cannula at night.

Incidentals

Paul very much appreciates foot/back massages and massage of R hand/arm.

Dermatologic Diagnosis:

Right forearm shave biopsy.

IRRITATED SEBORRHEIC KERATOSIS WITH SECONDARY CHANGES OF LICHEN SIMPLEX CHRONICUS.

12

Apraxia

Kim usually began my speech therapy session by having me blow through the magic whistle, which was proving to increase my lung power. If no cheating, which meant sealing my lips steadfastly around the tube. Leaking air was taboo. I took elaborate care to close every aperture that would mean a scant rehearsal, and never cheating by shortening my inhale on a second blow. What would be the point of cheating when your life depended on the correct performance? Five puffs only, but enough to exercise the lungs.

    Kim supervised with a connoisseur's diligence and egged me on to greater efforts. Once satisfied, she broached another subject—asking about my father, a fisherman whom war claimed in 1918. (He was blinded totally for a year, sight restored in one eye soon after.) Meandering dialogue was an exercise for me to learn to converse, struggling against the apraxia that clogged discourse from my otherwise nimble brain.

    For instance, this exchange.

    Kim: You say that your father never fished again after the war?

    Me: "Wanna."

"Try."

"Welllll...."

"You can."

"Enggglish!"

"Yes. You can do it."

"Whillll try."

"Go ahead."

"My fadder...."

"Wrong word."

"My fadder...."

"Wrong word again."

"My fadder...was black."

"Wrong word again, going afield too."

"My fadder...."

"Wrong word."

"My father was..."

"Yes. Continue."

"Can't."

At other times words decided to relent and became almost docile.

"My father."

"Bravo. You've done it."

"Thank God."

"Thank who you want."

"Him."

"Who?"

"Your father."

"Ah, it's time to go to physical therapy. Let me steer you up there."

My head ached with the effort. My mind was its usual spontaneous self, but only in its internal and existential pursuits. Normally sharp as a pin, I was a muddly, disheveled and powerless raconteur, the art of repartee refusing even my simplest overtures and disdaining my most elementary attempts to say anything at all. Obliterating what I said into a hopscotch of pidgin rigmarole.

No wonder I was the quiet man.

With a wisp of a smile, a hint of better things to come, Niele introduced the task of the day. "Climbing in and out of bed? How does that suit you?" I remained silent, employing my mute shrug which said, no problems so far.

"You mean someone helps you in and out of bed?"

I mimed an answer, which transcribed, said Carmen does all of that.

"Demonstrate, if you can."

I paused.

"Well. We have not got the whole day to squander."

I tried a word. "Carmen."

"You mean that without her help, you do nothing about it, rising and falling with the sun."

Nothing like a hint of sarcasm to get things off to a good start. I mimed yes. What else to do?

Niele freed me from my wheelchair onto the bed before me. I was in sitting position, the last refuge of a scoundrel.

"You look like you could sit like this forever."

I indicated yes. The next move was mine.

"Rise from your bed."

I did not budge.

Neither did she.

I thought, *Stalemate*. But she gently pushed me over and toppling, I lay prostrate before her in my lifelong sleeping position.

"Now get up. Or try."

I could not. I called Carmen to help, but there was no answer. Carmen was undoubtedly asleep in her own bed after a full night of looking after me.

"Get up now."

I was helpless.

"Swing your legs. Yes. Like that. Steady now. Try to push with your good arm."

I tried, but my body resisted.

"Harder. Push harder."

An inch, if that.

"Push as if you hated it."

I did, achieving the full weight of my body against my arm. Surely it would snap. I expected the arm might crack at any moment, and I would shriek with agony. Instead the arm sufficed to raise me from a half-reclining position to another posture which I had never experienced before, a position of self-mastery from which I maneuvered myself to semi-sitting up, and then in what seemed like ease, the arm clicked straight and I righted myself fully in a triumph of glory.

"See, I told you so. Never say die."

Niele was right. I must never say *that*—even when I have given up. I will not betray myself as an interloper, a mute vagabond. I shall go on and on, going to bed and a second later getting up, just for the pleasure of *independence*, driven to it by Niele's golden exultation of "Stand up and be counted."

"Good morning," said Francis, "and the Florida luck to you. I propose two exercises today—leg press and recumbent bike. How's that suit you?"

I murmured something that could be taken as "Hi" but also counted as "I" or even "Fine." He was by now used to intuiting my words without being capable of hearing them.

We set to the leg press. Lying supine, I felt the full force of the weight on my lower limbs and attempted to bend its sublime impassivity to my will. Nothing happened. The weight resisted my foolish efforts to budge it. This was so different from my first days with Francis, working out with 5 pound weights strapped on each ankle, brisk walks, kicking rubber balls, and tossing darts.

"Certainly not as impressive as necrotizing fasciitis," said Francis, for whomever was listening in (quite a few interlopers it always seemed).

I made a sound of faint demurral, say a *pshaw* or a *nooo*, but he pressed on with his romantic vision of my future status.

"Why, he'll one day lift 180 pounds, and we'll have to have a new machine installed to make him feel at ease."

I again made the sound of protest, the *pshaw* which denoted my disagreement, but he sailed through it, devoted to my cause.

"Watch him progress," he said to the admiring throng. "You never will believe it."

The gathering dispersed to other pursuits, and Francis confronted me with "How did you do?"

I did my best to tell him, but ended up burying him in my lingo of the Hottentots, *zume spum*, or some variant of non-useful sounds, brought to the forefront in this tragic phonetic condition I found myself in.

"Never say die," Francis pontificated, "even to your friends. Especially friends. I've learned that by heart. Now to the lighter assignment, the recumbent bike. If the weaker leg can stand it."

I did as he bade me, pressing gingerly with the aforementioned leg, easing onto the pedal inch by inch. All was well as I began to peddle the machine, slow at first, then faster, as my confidence grew and my heart calmed. Things were returning to normal again after my encounter with the leg press. (At which I had dismally failed.)

Francis always addressed me as if I was a whole man, instead of a man (if) whose brief attempts at language would make geniuses of all other persons in sight. I signaled I wanted to know something, which I did by tapping my skull and making an irresistible trilled cacophony both as a warning and apology for being mute to the least brilliant ideas. *Woe is me*, I wanted to say, in expectation of a policy change higher up in the ranks, the precincts of nonentity.

I could be ragged, spavined, and beaten to a pulp. But, of course, I am joking. Always I slept three hours to recover and felt better for it, although still puzzled by what people heard from me in moments when my syntax takes a rest and dwindles to an almost apprehensive iconography.

When alone, I grapple with commonplace stuff, such as one-handed toiletry—Adult Care is the cute name for it—and taking a shower, which chiefly denotes cleansing the genital area. Oh, for Carmen's purifying ablutions in that place. Instead I made do with imagination. Who next would touch that which dangles before me?

Meanwhile the food was good, rising to heights unexpected in such a place. Baked salmon with Bulgarian crayfish, cream puffs with mounds of extra icing. I heard rumor that a sensational new chef was ruling the roost and I wrote him accolades singing his praises. The result was even huger platefuls of anything my heart desired and my weight increased accordingly. Lucian, taskmaster of the scale, commented on my weekly weigh-in, "Watch it, Señor, they may be sending you home with a message: Cannot constrain him further."

13

Rigor and Zeal

Across the street, high on the brink of a multi-tiered office building, a half-moon of commemorative figures, all astronomical, sat on the roof and when the sun shone on them, they glistened with preternatural life like a disjoined palindrome, deployed for life, one by one. To my dismay, I was never able to identify the figures.

On Sunday afternoons, I wheeled with Carmen's help downstairs, through the gymnasium, that palace of therapeutic pleasure that was my thoroughfare during the week, exiting the main doors to savor the outside grounds of Gardens Court. Which were restful, calming, and hot. I preferred to sit in the shade, though we often wheeled through the walks for a change of pace. Carmen would have preferred constant sunlight, but she deferred to me, the former connoisseur of sunshine now avoiding serious rays.

When we returned from our siesta, in the sun or half-sun, it was through the same castle of varieties as before, sprinkled with a touch of mid-day light. The fitness machines silent, but somehow dressed down for the weekend. In some ways it was a ghostly place, dedicated to the old, its every gesture presuming senescence with each bout of health.

When rain interfered or when I was too tired to go for an afternoon outing, we played a game. I full-voiced, for once.

"Halt. Who Goes There?" (Carmen)

"A vowel." (Me)

"Advance vowel and be recognized."

"Coming."

"Who is vowel?"

"Powell."

"Otherwise."

"Did you say dirty?"

"What?"

"Something dirty."

"Who? Me?"

"Yes. You."

"I Powell."

"So you said."

"Was it that."

"Shit."

"Oh, I know."

For a month and a half in speech therapy, I have been saying my prayers to a tendentious litany of "Pucker your lips" (a favorite phrase of Kim's) and then, "smile wide." Followed by a benediction, "ooo—eee."

Then a burp of mine—usually anyway.

Always followed by "Puff out cheeks and hold 5 seconds." Then, "Stick out your tongue and hold 5 seconds." And 6 more classic injunctions. I rather enjoyed the ritual, putting me in the mind of old schoolboy grimaces, though not as inventive by far.

Today was different, however. Kim produced a book called *Secrets* by Rhonda Byrne. Neither the book nor its author rang a bell. The book was now mine—a gift, I was to understand. I awaited Kim's explanation.

This is a book about authors, she explained with a grin. They wanted a book, so they had one produced. Nonentities. For instance, she read a list of names: "Bob Proctor, Joe Vilale, John Assaraf, Dr. John Demartini, Dr. Denis Hartley…"

I interrupted to ask how many doctorates had been given to the worthy gentlemen. "The eye tells all," she answered. "Look and you will see!"

"Why?"

"To warn you about giving advice to people who have not asked for it."

"Why me?"

"To purge my shelves of unwanted books. For example…" She read aloud from some anonymous text. "Visualize checks in the mail." Nothing happened. It was a relief to get back to linguistic exercises.

This bizarre book was issued by my own publisher. Why I was made the recipient of such a gift I shall never know. A spoof? A practical joke? Kim was wittier than this by far. I was glad to get back to *Pah*, *Tah*, and *Kah*, five times each, slowly and clearly.

When time was up, she merrily delivered me to Niele's province, leaving me with her typical cordial good-bye, "See you tomorrow. At the same time."

"Hot towel?" Niele's offer was irresistible, followed by weights and measures, which weren't. The sooner I fell into my beauty sleep the better.

The difference between the therapists was impressive. Kim wanted quick fire responses within a second or two, while Niele and Francis tested you with an assignment to perform and left you to get on with it in your own time. Different horses for different courses, all ideal for the task at hand. The result was that each day I left therapy bone-tired and took every spare minute to recover. All three worked hard on this victim of their choosing, and deep down I thanked them for putting me through my paces with such rigor and zeal.

One morning was different. For once, Niele was absent, and the woman in charge was Tea, who announced for starters, "I'm going to teach you how to take your trousers down."

I answered as best I could, which demanded a short syllable, "I know," disguised thanks to my condition, as "No."

Tea was amazed. "Show me then."

I did.

"Then show me how you put them on."

Again I complied, despite mounting difficulty, one-handed it was especially hard to secure the final cinch. Finally I triumphed, making Tea gasp with wonder.

"You did it!"

"Hi."

"What?"

---- ----- I said nothing.

"Let me see you do it again."

---- ---- I refused point blank.

Tea walked away muttering.

I wondered at such behavior, but put it down to oblivious caregivers, who did not know how best to help but persisted in doing *something* nonetheless. I began to wonder if one unacquainted with my bizarre condition—nonverbal on the outside, yet verbally dextrous within—could learn ever how to cope with so enigmatic a being on the premises. In the end, I entrusted my fate to luck and serendipity, the first rather more than the second.

I wondered who would be next in line to put me through my exhausting paces. To my relief, it was Francis, fresh from golf and anxious to begin despite my shortness of breath.

14

Some Penitent Angel

"How's tricks, Trix?"

No response.

"I thought so. Who's been upsetting you?"

No response.

"I see. Niele?"

"No."

"Then who?"

No response.

"I see. Very young?"

No response.

"Understand. Want some recumbent bike?

My interior voice said *that would be wonderful and thank you for everything.*

Those who try to convict me of being deaf as a post have no idea of the rich interior life I inhabit. Bright black, if you must choose a color to reveal the status of it, as if left by some penitent angel. I was having it all, as scissors purred over me to free me of dross. Tiny teeth punctured my flesh as if liberated from bondage. And I alone to save thee.

Francis said that at some time he wanted to see what lay far to the north.

I murmured assent.

"I beg your pardon? Did you say something?"

Only to bleeding heart.

"Did you at long last say something?"

Only to keep body alive.

"Which was?"

Nothing, nothing.

15

The Physiatrist

Paul's physiatrist stopped by today (Dr. Lochner). Dr. Lochner would like Paul to be using his right hand and arm as much as possible for daily activities. You have probably noticed Paul is using his left hand to do pretty much everything, and ignoring his right hand/arm. We need to encourage Paul to push himself to use his R hand and arm as much as possible. Even though it's easier and quicker and less frustrating to do things with his left hand.

OT Update:
Paul has (dependent on muscle fatigue) good clenching/grasping ability in his right hand. He is not able (yet) to fire the muscles to open up his right hand. So if he picks something up, he can't let it go. Unfortunately because Paul has an old pacemaker (implant 1985), the therapists can't use electrical stimulation to wake up those muscles. That means Paul's going to have to work extra hard to use the arm to get results. The therapists are using vibration to stimulate the muscles externally.

Hand Brace Update:

To encourage Paul to use his hand more, the brace no longer needs to be worn during the day. It's important that he still wear the brace when he is sleeping to prevent contracture.

However, if Paul is awake (for example, watching TV at night) it is important that he keep the hand/palm open and as flat as possible. One way to do this is to put the TV tray in front of him and have his hand flat on the tray. If he is watching TV and he can't keep his hand open—it's curling up/contracting—best to put on the brace.

1. Turn to right and cough.
2. Eat small portions.
3. Inspect mouth for residue.

Things Paul should be encouraged to do with his right arm/hand (He may need to be verbally cued). Feel free to add more!

- Paul now has an extender on the right side wheelchair brake. He can use his right hand to put the brake on and off.

- Reach for Kleenex. (He may not be able to pull it out of the box, but ok to just attempt.) You'll need to put the box down low, he has trouble lifting his arm against gravity.
- Bear weight on the right arm and hand when transferring out of bed to wheelchair and vice versa. (Retraining his body to utilize, not ignore, the right arm).

Things Paul should be encouraged to NOT do:

- Cheat and move his right hand with his left hand (Paul often grasps the right hand with his left to move it across the body). Cue him to make the right hand and arm move independently. Independent, self-directed movement is essential to regain and improve control of these arm muscles.
- Take off right side wheelchair brake by reaching across with left arm

16

No Life at the Equator

Among scores of people never to be seen again there were one or two, or perhaps six or seven, worth committing to memory. For instance there was the bellow of a native African or the abrasive and faintly hostile voice of her successor. Gone, alas, like youth, too soon. There was the sweetheart who referred each morning to me as "Mah man" without going further. And the exquisite creature who waddled like a duck and specialized in getting prescriptions wrong. To this bevy of beauties, from the depths of the Congo or from the plains of the palsied Bahamas, I send the futile greetings of a determined survivor.

Not to mention Penny, the magistrate dominatrix of the whole show. A physician's assistant, Penny had class. She managed the medications, oversaw my lab reports, and, always meticulous, had me x-rayed more than once to check for pneumonia. To my dismay, I once sprayed a mess of my lunch over her in a sneeze, which I am now uncontrollably wont to do. In return, she pointedly asked me about my health whenever our paths crossed. In detail. She cared, people said, a little too much and too little about the paperwork which festooned the main office.

Mary-Beth was the senior nurse on our floor, a curvaceous blonde with a loud, intemperate voice. Mary-Beth had a grown-up daughter who kept her poor, she said, and unable to pursue an exotic career. She was a demon on the approach, heard from a hundred yards away. You had to get ready with all your guns blazing. Her visits lasted no longer than a minute, except if you were one of her favorites, in which case she might linger a quarter of an hour, especially if business on the floor was slow. Mary-Beth had an eye for men and men had an eye for her. Why, once she even kissed me for sticking up for her in a dispute. She remains in my mind as an epitome of a breed of righteous women, astute, stentorian, and warm.

17

Jessica and Sayeed

Jessica was a fully qualified RN whose main occupation was trouble-shooting the various ailments afflicting the resident population from time to time, such as non-delivery of pills, a need to escape the clutches of the system, the calls for a dentist or a blocked toilet. She was an endlessly beneficent woman who said that the only woman who could replace her was our Liz, whom she admired with a redeemer's kiss.

    She was a housewife too, with husband and children. Jessica thrived on work, and duly brought me my pills, contributing the sobriquet "sweetheart" to my cause. She suffered from an unmentionable disease which made her gain weight.

    All things considered, Jessica was a powerhouse of a woman, whose desire for influence bespoke some *folie de grandeur*, as the French would say, but not when she could do every job so well. Each morning she gave me a peck on the cheek to keep my spirits alive during the worst months of my stay. Perhaps pecks on the cheek like that restored faith in an old dog worn in the teeth. I even suspected Jessica's able hand in the brittle cart squawk of my poached egg delivery each morning at breakfast.

An unsolved mystery was the puzzle of my egg delivery; in the beginning eggs arrived in singles or doubles, or triples, in unpredictable combinations of one boiled, two not, two boiled, one not, and so on. Some fiendishly erratic ovoid operator behind the scenes? Within two weeks, the inconsistency disappeared, but to my relief not the eggs themselves. Perhaps a dying mother had interceded on my breakfast's behalf.

I don't remember perfectly. Perhaps it's merely a relic of my childhood athletics, but I vividly recall this *mis-en-scène*. Francis had me standing on one leg, swinging my weak leg back and forth to his rhythm and I was singing. It happened only once. I was not much of a singer (especially of Scottish ballads), but on this occasion, fired by my elation of being able to do the trick at all, I let myself go. Besides, the day was late, everyone had gone home and the only person left was the therapist with the most refined manner I had ever seen.

Sayeed was an expatriate of Egypt, whose wife lived elsewhere for some undivulged reason. Such an arrangement did not hamper Sayeed's smooth rhetoric one jot, however, and I still remember his polite knocks at the door of my lair when he replaced Francis who took weekends off. Sayeed had a congenial word for everybody, always in perfect English, and always suave manners.

"Good morning," Sayeed greeted me, "I hope my intrusions will not disturb you, but I see that Francis is off and I am available for whatever takes your fancy. My hours are from ten until three o'clock." Unfortunately for Sayeed, I usually kept Sundays free for work on this book. But on this particular day, Sayeed struck it lucky.

This was going to be a switch from Francis, whose manner was diffident, though autocratic. Sayeed's halcyon tone was softer, almost genial, knowing, maternal. *Tic, Tac*, he purred as my marching orders changed from hesitant flounderings to confident steps forward, no longer in danger of crossing my feet. *Correct with high stepping*, Sayeed recommended, and reconsider before going further. I did, wondering why the simple art of walking demanded such intimate rigmarole as this. Then I remembered my debilitated condition.

Now I had two experts taking my fate upon themselves, pronouncing judgment, *ad lib*. Sayeed liked to stand closer to me than Francis and to walk more quickly. *Now, keep it straight.* I pushed forward, hoping to please as they marched me forward, pupil of two masters, master of none. I soon ended this dual master experiment, denying Sayeed all his shibboleths. To dissuade him, I even reconfigured my armory of answering tricks (*hi, fine*) to include for the first time the tentative hand signal indicating *I don't know what to think*, or *I don't know if I'm available*. *Comme si, comme ça*, as Niele's people knew it.

This solemn avoidance of Sayeed's marching orders, *Tic, Tac*, disturbed him not at all. He happily went on in his tranquil nirvana, seemingly convinced that any people wishing to substitute my silence for talking should be damned.

I last saw Sayeed when Carmen and I were returning from one of our visits to the outside grounds. He was at work with a patient in the otherwise deserted therapy room, scene of so many triumphs and disasters. To his toil he had added this girl with a broken arm, which she brandished like some trophy of a far distant war, patting it and calling it pretty names.

Could a man specialized on correcting someone's gait be of use a woman with a broken arm, I wondered. But there he was, with softly spoken noblesse oblige couched in his encouraging, soothing tone. Carmen and I passed on, dismissing what seemed an apparition from the Middle Ages, a broken warrior seeking help espied by two bystanders with things of their own to worry about.

Whatever. I wish Sayeed well, not least his prowess as a runner (about which I had glowing reports). I miss him as a friend never made, largely to my overcommitment in three months of rehab. Simply put, I was over-engaged.

I was growing accustomed to various people knocking at my door, one after the other, flower-sellers, doctors, Lucian's requests for weight, interviewers, and the like. Some, mainly meal deliverers, barged in as if there was no tomorrow, and left without a single word, which was their brutish way of doing things.

Interviewers—also known as social workers—I had no truck with, knowing the breed by heart. For one in particular I rescued a firm one-word dismissal—OUT. Thus enforcing my rule against conversation. I hasten to explain that I kept the one-word rule for emergencies; OUT, SCRAM, and BEGONE in the main for this refined version of obloquy.

After dismissing the first would-be social worker with OUT, I repeated the same to another the following week. Then came a third, more palatable, to whom I said "Shem valu hudnita, bur ev sigrioner vasili toto." (The Choctaw version of: *You'll not be capable of understanding what I'm saying!*)

About a week later came another tap on the door, using without abusing it. This time it was a real beauty, in the radiant class of my friend Kim, though a tad younger. I welcomed her with open arms, as they say, though attending to my inner voice that said *Be careful, you know what happened last time.*

She was a Colgate graduate, a classy blonde with an endearing Spanish accent, though as American as apple pie. Much travelled, I thought. Maybe she's a Beckett fan, or at last a Proustian.

Throwing caution to the wind, I hastened to inform this gem of my lineage, but her face fell at once. I had forgotten my status as an unfathomable. She recovered, begging pardon for her lapse in attention. I repeated myself, ignoring my special status as a man whose brain thinks clearly but who is deprived of comprehensive language apart from *Hi, Scram,* and *Out,* and other such monosyllabic gibberish I might lay claim to. What I said to her, to calm her down, was *Chi mot hastan,* verily, in literate English, *I'm very happy to meet you.*

Muttering some pretext, she was gone from my life forever, leaving behind her faint smell of patchouli. I had not gotten to first base with her, not even made verbal contact. *Oh me miserum.* I was so dejected I could not even say my mantra, *Hi, Scram*—to the rest of my dismal destiny. I was alone in a telephone box, receiver down.

When I at last began to function again, throwing all caution to the winds, I visited the toilet (which was soon to figure in another episode of my tormented life) and then opened the door to the outside halls hoping to catch a whiff of her, but I was arrested by a message pinned to my door. Whether in spite or in sympathy, I know not, but clearly invented to demoralize me utterly.

Mr. West is sleeping
Recovering from Physical Therapy
Please open door quietly
Thank you!

I reached for the nearest V-8 and drank my fill.

18

One Trick

There is one exquisite trick I have mastered, and that is to open a can of V-8. Take an ordinary fork, apply its teeth under the pop-top flange, then twist. Make sure you have clamped your fingers around the base of the can, immobilizing the can with your thumb (your defunct hand will do). Then flip up the top and allow the can to open up its treasure to the world outside.

The result should be a pop and the contents should be free to consume. If a loud pop does not happen, you have done it wrong and should start again. The pop is crucial to the can's resonant performance and should in no way impede the completion of the opening. Or the ceremony, if you wish to be liturgical.

I have opened five hundred V-8's now, in this very way, failing with maybe half-a-dozen, either with a badly angled fork or with a recalcitrant can, in which circumstance there is no hope at all freeing the contents. In this case you plump for ice cream or the little known Tizer (a British beer, bottled).

All this is not to damage in any way the secure reputation of other challenging containers, bottles, and devices. I have a select list of favorites, among these, Thick and Easy, also known also as Hydrolyte or Nectar Consistency water. It is impossible to open if you are one-handed. Otherwise, the taste is fine, with a bright tinge of lemon (I almost wrote lemur), quickening up the drink.

Another damnation of my newly left-handed existence is the merciless appliance into which I attempt to corral writing paper. A clipboard's clamp is genial, except for the obtuse bracket which prevents me from feeding the paper up to the clamp's hilt. With never any one around to help.

Ah, the charm of being a one-handed man in a wheelchair, with all the money on what's behind you and what is gaining on you. Ah, the perils of always careening into things or of being typecast as a backward man, unable to make his own bread and butter or even to speak his verbally handicapped prayers.

A truly minor trouble is the wheelchair dismount if one has one's *cojones* jammed in sideways, squeezed and poxed in all sorts of non-imaginative ways sufficient to turn a healthy man into a splendid catamite. Those involved in the puzzle will recognize the symptoms. This squeezing of the balls guarantees the race the production of a breed of detesticulated men likely to inherit the earth or be invaded by Martians hot to trot among paradises lost.

    Fear not the Martian invaders, but for heaven's sake keep the home fires burning. Abolish all wheelchairs in the interest of the handicapped and others like them, denatured into despair. Fear not, but the helping hands promising to eject us from our comfortable chairs. Thousands have had their privates crushed in the vise of comfort, I am only one voice raised in protest. Many have gone before, denatured before their time, meat on the waste carpet of history with hardly a murmur save one agonized shriek as their balls bite the dust.

19

Anti-Spasticity

Among Niele's gifts was a prosthesis called an anti-spasticity brace, intended for someone such as I whose hand had reduced itself to a clenched and useless fist of fingers. It was a webbed device to stretch and separate my fingers.

What was this like to wear? Predominantly a feeling of my hand being overweight from feeling bowed over with its plastic bulk. Not heavy *per se*, but unwieldy and ponderous, constricting, rigid. In short, I did not like it on my arm.

That was the black side of it. The other side was the good I was doing for my fingers, growing them up to save them from being lifeless appendages and freshening them up for living again. Or so I dreamed. The real truth was that the device did not naturally grow fingers out of nothing. Despite wearing it faithfully, I half-hoped some rehabilitative infidel would take over and make me feel justified in taking it off, resentful and disdainful as I felt.

No, new fingers do not grow on trees, or more precisely, do not resume their natural tendency just for being asked to do so, like some teenager invited to a party. They have to be cajoled into it, growing envious of functional parts of the body, with neurons that happily go about their traditional business of making the body enter into bountiful partnerships of making the whole fructify.

How wonderful, then, to feel the first stiffening of life in the old carcass, the first intonation of a running spring, not fulsome you understand, but a trickle, a little runnel or two running downward past the wrist. Not much to get excited about, but to one habituated to zero feeling in a hand, a limitless treasure, if only the dimension of a tadpole.

We are said to be recuperative if proven alive, but whatever the facts, the feeling needs to be there—if not of a tadpole then of a spirit ditty of no tone.

If you need extra support for this hypothesis, consult the black arts of the witch of Endor whose word is law among heathen races. From her, learn to estimate the significance of a tadpole to the benighted beings born to be saved.

I rest my case among the tadpoles. If not they among the lightest of beings, say those who haunt the daylight with their wispy crenellates, not real but as if a linnet's wing. Coming back to life, I rage against all those who have able bodies in their arms.

20

We'll Walk

"We'll walk," said Francis, as he has said hundreds of times before in his baldly matter of fact tone, "for a change." A faint laugh proves his point, and I remember how we had progressed from walker to cane, and from there to a slight tether which he fastened around my torso so he could restrain me if I began to fall.

    We walked, but there was something different about it. I no longer favored my right foot, which is to say I no longer tripped. I was making progress, and he knew. I no longer dreaded the end of the hall, the wall that suddenly disappeared as I walked blindly beyond it, testing my balance as I navigated through empty space. I sailed past with newfound confidence, secure with Francis reining in my tripping motion of old. No longer was I a raw recruit, reeling from pillar to post, but a competent pedestrian, able to walk. I had come through his vale of tears—I was proud.

    Now Francis summoned me to attempt a miracle, "the stairs." I stared at him, incredulous, certain that his customary bonhomie had failed and been replaced by an alter ego, demanding, brusque, and mildly insane.

"A dozen steps up, a dozen steps down. Go on, you can do it. Think of Trafalgar. Francis Drake and Nelson. Think big."

I had no memory of how to step up stairs, but surely I had traversed thousands in my time on earth. This competence gone, like youth, too soon. Warily, I set about the allotted task, which to my complete amazement I managed perfectly.

God or his minions must have been with me. No missteps, no stumbles, no crossed legs, no disaster. Francis applauded me with wild cries. "You've done it! Ten out of ten! How did you do that?"

Casting around for a syllable, I found "Can't say" interred in a shrug, a motion sufficing where a word should do.

"Do it again, please."

I complied, still without error.

"Fantastic!"

I collapsed onto a convenient chair, panting for breath and anxious never to repeat the feat. Ever.

"Come on, it's time for coffee. You master of the steps."

I did as told, master of myself for all occasions.

21

In a Bauhaus Sort of Way

"Let me show you something," Kim said, with roguish intonation, "Something you won't need barring the catastrophic."

I had no idea what she had in mind, perhaps a grand tour of the upstairs ward where the abandoned were permanently housed. Kim understood my taste for the ghoulish and the exotic.

Instead she showed me a room nearby, spic and span. Clearly it was not used much and I figured it was—or had been—a conference room, overstated and rather old-fashioned in a Bauhaus sort of way.

"Welcome to the transition room," she said. "It is a room where people get ready for life in the world outside. I very nearly said afterlife. I must have been dreaming."

I had not noticed her slip, too engrossed with the odd made to measure tone of the place, the way each piece of the table furniture was just so, everything predictable, no surprises, so standard, so subfusc. This was a room for the newly handicapped.

"Take care," she said, "not to touch anything. The whole room has been designed to have no ifs and no surprises—the people it serves must have nothing that makes them feel ill at ease, nothing out of the ordinary to throw them into a panic.

I marveled at this disconcerting variety of reality, obliged to satisfy the masses. I was in the presence of an oxymoron of taste, an *ignis fatuus* of neuter caliber. Those whose generic taste was not gratified by the display had nowhere to go on the planet. On the whole, I felt this spectacle was for the birds, as people say, mindless extravagance in the interest of nobody at all. I very nearly threw up at its neutrality and I imagined the whole room as a tranquil blank despite what she had said about its virtues.

It was a room where I would never come by free will, but would fall shrieking at the brink, crying aloud not to be allowed to enter among its vitreous non-entity.

My lackluster response chastened Kim a little without changing her mind. She still sentimentally envisioned the ancient of days queuing up to be spoonfed, and I decided to let the matter rest. Years ago, my ancestors had satisfied themselves with thinking a plate was a platter with nothing more to be said. Ah, for those venerable, prolix days when we were gratefully uninitiated.

"You don't look very pleased."

My rebuttal was limited, as ever. A mumble disguised as a grunt, got up to resemble a peacock. Any response will suffice, given my condition, though my response did improve from time to time—maybe a syllable disguised as a sound got up as a nightingale. When nobody understands you whenever you try to talk, the field is yours, Gunga Din, and will always be so.

You might have shown some interest."

I wanted to tell her at length, pausing for breath every five minutes or so, fine-tuning my English to an absurd degree, spelling out my resentment as so many old souls being bilked (or whatever the process is called nowadays in the time of insufficient plenty), but modesty forbids, and so does beauty, and the spavination.

22

Underground Man

I come now to that part of my life when I called myself the Underground Man. The Underground Man began his stealthy career in the vacant dark hours between waking up and having breakfast. The passing of time took the form of one hour of exercise for languid hand, one hour for weakened arm. This left both speech and leg out of the equation, both of which, in my god-given therapist-filled state, I regarded as already taken care of.

As follows. Hand work half an hour with my left forcing the right to unstick its clenched fingers and loosen it up. Then half an hour of flexing the wrist. I spent the other hour stretching limp forearm and extending my elbow, which was painful but useful, restoring half of the range required to reach.

I hoped to self-remedy—Underground, as it were—drooping hand and arm to normal use. Two hours a morning of supplementary calisthenics, preceding enormous breakfast of poached eggs and sausages. A fine repast for an amateur athlete. My crack team of elite therapists to follow.

I busied myself with this private routine, noting each little improvement with the unrestrained joy of an amateur. A gradual uncurling of the right hand, no longer inert; an ever-so-slow release of the fingers. These things brightened my day even before it began. To be true, the experts labored much harder than I, but I worked with comparable effect.

Inch by inch, I watched my fingers' motions (or not), and even if the latter happened there was the gloomy, aborted feeling to be amused with. Better luck next time, I told myself, there is always tomorrow to turn the fertile fingers to grow and thrive again. As before, a million years ago. It is not good to play nature against itself.

In these spare hours, I encountered visions in space and time. Not for the usual hallucinatory reasons, but because I pleased myself with what I saw. Such as supposing a cayman, a crocodile, or a Flying Fortress, an autogyro. Ah, you say, it's only a matter of degree then, this refusal to believe what the eye sees it. But not so fast, the human mind pleases itself, whatever the consequences. Especially the mind of a novelist.

I believe in variety. It is the source of literature and many other apparitions, not least the werewolf and the Frankenstein monster. One so easily gets bored with crocodiles and Flying Fortresses.

23

Trysts

Thoughts to amuse oneself in the night. Have you noticed that elementary lovers succumbed by self-induced frenzy choose to keep private the most cherished encounters of their love trysts? So the resounding thwack on the rump, a sort of bumpkiss in extremist, cannot be shared any more than can the angle of a penis. Such stimulants lovers keep to themselves, quietly longing for *folie de grandeur* to quicken their naked appetites.

On the other hand, well-versed experienced lovers will mount their desires like a display of mating bison, asking or receiving as good as they are getting. It all depends on who is doing what to whom at a given moment. These are the times when sheer lust opens its door wide for enough bone-chilling grandiosity to make the angels sing. Who profits from such escapes? No one in the long run. People, testing their partner's mettle, fall back, sooner or later craving for more on the brink of appetitive desire.

Clearly, those whose lust is so grand desire the impossible, a kingdom of non-stop which expends partners just as they receive their final climax. They desire to die in one supreme act of unblemished annihilation. Thus my thoughts in this palace of denied pleasure, this wen of mutilated souls.

I was an ass man, also a tit man. I like both, truth told, and I marvel at the universe providing us with such estimable fodder. Things might have been different, with nowhere to put a long-troubled erection. Think of it, a universe full of men beating off their pleasure in the sight of an impervious god. Not a virgin in the whole damned place.

The lame hand was dry. I looked at it again; my dry hand. Sometimes the feeling was of blood pouring through the limb, a muddy blood trying to pass from one station to the next. The hand felt hard and brittle, not mobile at all. It felt old and denatured, the hand of a dead man, close to and certain to soon arrive on the chopping block of history.

Then sensations, as if a downpour of water—*blood?*—to the floor. Things just could not be this bad. Abrupt change from some stagnant fluid to one of rushing liquid, and then to a sodden, harmonic feeling, which made me feel much better, though a little peeved. Why was it taking the hand so long to go through successive changes? I would just watch like the Gods from above with my head held high. My countenance restored, I lay down to sleep but the hand kept me awake with a quick tremor jiggling the bedframe. At least, I told myself, something is going on. I am not dead yet at any rate.

After a while, I sensed a new motion, not so brisk but tenuous, not too solid, not brittle at all, but light-fingered as a pianist playing on the harmonica, fingering an absent melody. It was not me unless I was playing by proxy, but I felt beyond accidental proof that my hand was moving for an hour or two.

24

Bemused As I Often Am

I am having a strange sensation in the hand; it feels as if I hold a handful of keys. I greet visitors with *How Now Brown Cow*. It sounds like *Hu Nu Bu Cu*, which goes nowhere fast. Does this mean I'm getting better? Or worse? Something is going on, I know not what it is. But Niele is determined to prevail and I don't want to leave half-done. Best to begin as you mean to go on. Message received and understood.

Bemused as I often am, I see no great appeal in hanging on for the sake of it. Better to give up the ghost and travel to that land from whose bosom no travelers come back. All the way to heaven, there to become a budgerigar like the boy in the Japanese folk tale. The Romans preserved their ashes without inscribing the names on their funerary urns. The beginnings of personality rest here, the cult, and all that goes with it. I'd be an unrecorded Roman.

I had rather have been a baboon or a carbide lamp or even a lion in the long grass than be a Roman identified. Or a thing Brezhnev on the plains of Asia or an angry catfish. Or a Puritan wheelmonger complaining about the water supply. Best to provide your own parachute.

For the first time, it appears, we thought of money and decided to cut back, and opted to lessen Carmen, who was the most costly, and found Beryl Walker who was cheap. She was lazy, fat, and garrulous, much given to sleep at the most inappropriate times, and actually nodded off while reading. A poor substitute to Carmen's new half-time arrangement. Carmen took her punishment like a man. There was always tennis to go back to.

Beryl, in her sluggish way, was cheerful to have around, slow to take offence and capable of asking prosaic questions without warning—*Do you miss your grandparents?* This to an 81-year old man. After a while you got used to her elementary diction and learned how to seek arcane meanings in whatever she said, just to pass the time. In this way, you could descend to her level without feeling embraced as an unworthy. Besides, she could understand little of what I said (my fault, as I told her repeatedly). She found it difficult to believe that a grown man made such a mess of his native language. We soldiered on in a slovenly fashion, believing that all good things must end, and the sooner the better.

Until the day, taken up short with a dose of Colace to the infernal regions below, I happened to need assistance in wiping myself down. I summoned Beryl from sleep (from wherever she pursued her classical studies). She was slow in responding to my call. I gave up waiting, and was just addressing myself when she arrived breathless and flummoxed as the rickety commode gave way and I found myself descending once again to the floor, toilet-seat in hand. Beryl made a feeble palsied fare-the-well touch to my vanishing rear end. I was again down among the dead men, vainly trying to steady myself against the toilet's tidal bulk, knees crossed, first to go, then the force of my body. I had fallen. It took the hands of four nurses to restore me to the upright position I prefer.

The last I saw Beryl she was clasping her misshapen hands as if she already knew the decision of the board of nurses on her conduct. I felt sorry for her. However, only a little bit. She had let me drop in the prime of my life and I would not forget.

There followed a flurry of red tape concerning who had done what to whom, and I was the one party innocent. Injuries to my right leg proved painful at the outset though superficial. And of course the phones rang themselves to death. There was a flurry of medicos bearing x-ray equipment, slight though my injuries had been.

As for Beryl, a covey of nurses put paid to her as the guilty party and she was not heard from again. Back to Carmen, expensive as she was. We played word games again with not a mention about what had happened, she was more open about the tennis matches, her husband and family politics. It was good to be back with Carmen, her body rubs and her brisk tones of command: *Roll over, Mister West, we'll do the body now and see if the fungus has visited us again.*

The nurses overflowed with good nature, making allusions to Beryl both sexist and scandalous. I didn't dissuade them, thinking that the less I said, the sooner it's mended. Besides, there was so much to do. There was talk of going home at last after three months in rehab, and I now realized I would miss the place, despite its foibles. There were times a rush of sensibility overran me, in which I thought the best is yet to come—yet I longed to preserve so many things—my therapists, my aides and nurses, even the man who came to weigh me weekly. I was what John Bunyan called Mister Facing-both-ways.

I turn now to the variety of fish which crossed my plate during my three month stay, some once only, some every week, some never, but imagined into being. Give me sin again, I said, whatever the expense. Cod always for me as if it were nectar. Pollock, the fish used in sandwiches along with Anchovies, Albacore, Halibut, Salmon, Striped Bass, Trout, and Bluefish.

I exemplify. Mackerel, Atlantic Chinook, Coho, Greenland Halibut, Catfish, and Flounder. They represent 100 grams of fatty acid per fish. You must hear me obsess on Flaxseed oil, Ground Flaxseed, Walnut oil, Chopped walnuts, Canola oil, hoping to craft the perfect diet for everyone, sinful as salmon.

Amid the surfeit of fish and fries, the thing that made my heart sing was dessert. And they were plentiful. Never tell a patient he is to be without sweets. Never tell this one anyway. I could list all alphabetically, but that would be too staid. So I introduce higgledy-piggledy to expose the delight of dessert at random in no discernible order. That this method, perhaps fractal, may actually concede a pattern in some cases has occurred to me, but I am not a mathematics professor, just a man who likes his sweets sweeter, especially when mooning about in rehab and waiting for the axe to fall.

We begin with Apple Turnover, Apple Pie (not a salubrious start), Cream Puff (heavenly), Lemon Meringue Pie, Cheesecake, Vanilla Pudding, Silk Pie, Pecan Pie, Chocolate Cannolis, Key Lime Pie, Vanilla Pudding, Black Forest Cake, Banana Cake, Lemon Bar, Chocolate Éclair, Coconut Cake, Banana Cream Pie, Pumpkin Pie, Black and White Pudding, Pound Cake, Peach Crisp, Brownie, Chocolate Cake, Cherry Pie, Bread Pudding, Cheesecake, Peach Pie, Angel Food Cake, Blueberry Pie, Cinnamon Baked Pears, Peach Pie, Rice Pudding, Pound Cake, Peach Cobbler, Peanut Butter Pie.

I could go on listing things just for the spirit of listing them. Beyond entertaining myself with reams of lists, nothing was more tonic than reflection on my university days, capped by the pinnacle year in New York City that was a pageant, irresistibly luring me back to what I always think of as the land of

Stravinsky, Faulkner, Einstein, Santayana, Wallace Stevens, plane-designer Kelly Johnson, and the great swing bands from Basie to Goodman.

Were I to start naming famous cricketers—Verity, Grace, Hollies, Truman, Sutcliffe, Pope, Copson, and the rest—it would get me through the day, no doubt about it, But what is the point? So I vow not to list any more, charming and stimulating as it can be.

Having swiftly (all by myself!) clambered out of bed, I found it impossible to fit my bathrobe to my form, mainly the sleeves which I couldn't find. A fly buzzed my face. I couldn't find a pen, my glasses were missing. Still not deterred. Glasses finally came to hand, followed by the foolscap (paper), which I once again could not fit into my clipboard. What was I doing with foolscap anyway, a man with a bum writing hand? My hopes of literary fame petered out and I turned to face the wall so not to see my sheet of paper refusing to be subdued.

I sat up, tried to be succored by a glass of milk. The milk was off. By this time I was well and truly knackered. I cast around to do something other than write or endless puffing on the pipe furnished by Kim. I gave up.

Later that morning, I tried again. Better equipped, I attempted to write a line or two, but it was no use trying to think. The caregivers were at the prowl again with their chorus and blood-curdling calls as they prepared breakfast.

I reserved another day for the tale I needed to tell, the story of how paper refused to enter clipboard, and how I was writing—sort of—with my left hand (an awkward, busy, exhausting process bound to end in grief).

I would always be behind a sheet of paper, busy about nobody's business, buzzed by itinerant fly, speechless, with my left handed scrawl. The laughingstock of language, rejected by an edict that said I had been too long in the trade to signal for help with palsied hand. Intimately knowing the difference between the O and O+, that top-grade, was almost unbelievable.

I dote on precious things, like the soulless summoning bell on which my life depends as I ring for assistance getting dressed. Or the way no amount of one-handed riffling can make sheets of paper collate together in perfect order. Or nonsensical propositions such as: Have you ever made your way in the world by losing all your physical prowess? Doubtless your experience has not matched mine, but it will happen to you in the long run, whoever you are or claim to be. This is the law of entropy, changeable always and pervasive as hell.

I have lost many of my possessions, and not a few people. Some say it is the law of the jungle, but to me it is the law of the pure. When asked, "Where is the home for paupers?" Someone retorted, "The paupers have no home, their home is in the clouds."

Paupers such as I should not bother to cope much with niceties such as dealing with my curl of hair that wants to grow awry. Nonetheless, I asked Carmen to cut the sprig down, so as to restore my quiff to its proper seemly place among my silver hair, amidst the bulk of it. I use the word *bulk* advisedly, conscious of its majestic resonance when applied to such a fleeting thing as hair. There is nothing like an old fool to toy with.

Just to reassure you that all was all right, I append the medical report signed by Dandiya Rohit and Amad Safar—names to conjure with!—after one of my falls.

NORMAL RIGHT ELBOW.
BOTH VIEWS OF THE RIGHT ELBOW SHOW NO CHANGE TO INDICATE ANY TYPE OF FRACTURE DISLOCATION OR LYTIC OR BLASTIC LESIONS. NEITHER THE ANTERIOR OR POSTERIOR FAT PAD IS ELEVATED NOR IS THERE ANY OTHER SOFT TISSUE TRAUMA. THE HUMERUS RADIUS ULNA AND FOREARM VISUALIZED ARE INTACT.

Did I mention I was *still* relearning how to eat? Verify that the tray is consistent with the diet. ½ teaspoon bites only. Swallow. Make sure the patient has swallowed after every bite. Encourage the patient to swallow "hard." Alternate after one bite with one sip throughout the meal. No straws. Crush pills. Serve with applesauce. With liquid, sit upright at a 90-degree angle, preferably in a chair.

I would rather to eat tons of banana cake than obey what is spelled out in a cautionary pamphlet evangelizing the problem of urinary incontinence. To whit: *A resident's right to choose care can increase the risk of urinary incontinence. Choosing not to drink adequate fluids, not to treat urinary tract infections, or not to comply with toileting needs can result....* We know what comes next in this assembly of threats.

A threat clearly real as "53 percent of homebound elderly have a diagnosis of U.I." Poor suckers rummaging in God's handiwork for some smidgen of charity. *Protocols for Care*, declares one headline, suggesting that the long word of protocol will make the whole right again.

I couple banana cake with U.I. advisedly if recklessly. Combining the best with the worst has always been the thing to do. Besides, in this case, if these are the best and worst, they are merely the trifles (or truffles) on the edges of a true epidemic. Perhaps the two compliment in some weird way.

This is just one instance of taking the rough with the smooth. Into each life some rain must fall. There seems to be ample room for this idea, worthwhile for any god waiting in the wings to try experiments. I've always thought the concept of rain exceptional for a half-inferior god anyway, whose godliness seems a little lacking in brainpower.

Back to the wind and rain, whose progeny I might be. Someone who dotes so much on sweetmeats surely has something wrong with him. Or with a shuddering, soon to fall off piece of him. Lovers of cricket or of baseball—such as I—surely have something wrong somewhere in their makeup, or they would not care so much about results. Yet, if you do not care about these things, I recommend you attend the next game in hope of a good show.

25

Among the Valiant

Among the valiant people who worked in my behalf while I was in rehab, one is notably missing—my wife of 42 years, Diane Ackerman—to perform exquisite duty travelling to publicize her latest book, her 21st. The accompanying schedule records her numerous comings and goings, and the infrequent hours we spent together in the sterile room with two separate beds. We snatched time as we could, accompanied by tears of vexation and separation and harsh partings. Her fortitude during this period was a miracle to behold. She is a marvel of womanhood unsurpassed, especially considering my condition. Her vines have robust grapes.

26

Calendar

MONDAY, APRIL 11 Liz 9am-3pm Kim out of town PacerCheck at 10am with Kathy Patricia 3pm-8pm Carmen 8pm-7:30am, leave early for CPR class	"Mimi Geerges Show" XM satellite radio 2pm-3pm Eye on Books interview Host Bill Thompson 4pm-5pm
TUESDAY APRIL 12 Liz 7:30am-noon Patricia noon-5pm Diane 5pm-8pm Carmen 8pm-10am	Diane Leaves Reagan Airport 8:45am Arrives West Palm Beach 11:15am Phoner 2pm-3pm Point Reyes

Wednesday April 13 Carmen is staying until you go to speech therapy Liz 11-3 Patricia 3pm-8pm Carmen 8pm-10am	Diane Diane Rehm Show with host Katty Kay 11am-noon Leave for Miami 8am? Stay at hotel in Miami for the afternoon Books and Books Coral Gables 8pm-9:30pm home at midnight?
Thursday April 14 Carmen will stay until you go to speech therapy Diane 11 am-1 pm Patricia 1 pm- 8pm	Diane Event at Four Arts needs to be at Four Arts by 5pm (+ nap first?)
Friday April 15 Liz 8am-4pm Diane 4pm-8pm	

Saturday April 16 Patricia 8am-6pm Diane 6pm-STAYING OVERNIGHT!	
Sunday April 17 Patricia 10am-6pm Diane 6pm-8pm	
Monday April 18 Liz's mom (Maggie) is in town Patricia 8am-8pm Carmen 8pm-10am	Diane flies to Atlanta Leaves West Palm Beach 2:45pm Arrives Atlanta 4:36 pm
Tuesday April 19 Carmen will stay until you go to speech therapy around 9:30am Patricia 11am-8pm Carmen 8pm-10am	Diane <u>BUSY DAY</u> 9am-9:30 am Interview for The Midtown Review 10am-10:30am Radio WMLB "Conversations with the Voice of the Arts" 11:30am-noon Interview for Atlanta Arts Diane, cont.

	Radio 3pm-4:30pm "Paula Gordon Show" 7pm-8:30pm EVENT Margaret Mitchell House
Wednesday April 20 Carmen will stay until you go to speech therapy around 11am Patricia 11a-8pm Carmen 8pm-10am	Diane flies from Atlanta to New York Leaves Atlanta 2:40pm Arrives NYC 5pm Staying at the Warwick Hotel on 54th St
Thursday April 21 Carmen will stay until you go to speech therapy around 9:30am LIZ 11am-3pm Patricia 3pm-8pm Carmen 8pm-10am	Diane= Another Busy Day! 10am-11am/noon-3pm "Authors at Google" Talk, signing, and lunch 3pm drop by WW Norton for meet & greet/sign 75 books 7pm-8:30pm National Aphasia Association Event at Barnes and Noble on 82nd St

Friday April 22 Carmen will stay until you go to speech therapy Liz 11-8 8pm-8am	Diane 12:40pm-1pm WNYC Leonard Lopate Show Flight Departs LaGuardia 5:45pm West Palm Beach 8:42 pm

Saturday April 23
Carmen 8am-8pm
Diane 4pm-8pm
If Diane is still sick, Carmen will stay 'til 8pm
Terry overnight

Sunday April 24
Carmen 8am-4pm
Diane 4pm-8pm
If Diane is still sick, Carmen will stay 'til 8pm
Terry overnight

Monday April 25
Liz, Diane, Carmen overnight

Tuesday April 26
Carmen will stay until you go to speech therapy with Kim
Liz 11-4
(->Target for shoes, socks, aqua velva)

Diane 4pm-8pm Carmen 8pm-overnight
Wed. April 27 Carmen will stay until you go to speech therapy with Kim Liz 11-4pm Diane 4pm-8pm Carmen 8pm-overnight
Thursday April 28 Carmen will stay until you go to speech therapy with Kim Liz 11-4pm Diane 4-8pm Patricia 8pm-overnight
Friday April 29 Patricia will stay until you go to speech therapy with Kim. Diane will meet you at Kim's at 9:30am and stay to watch therapy with Niele/Francis Liz 3-8pm New Aide 8pm-overnight

Saturday April 30 Patricia 8am-8pm Diane 8pm-overnight
Sunday 5/1 Patricia 10am-8pm Carmn 8pm-overnight
Monday 5/2 Carmen will stay until you're ready to go to speech therapy Patricia 11am-6pm Diane 6pm-9pm Carmen 9pm-overnight
Tuesday May 3 Liz 11am-6pm Diane 6pm-9pm Aide 9pm-10am
Wed. May 4 Aide will wake you up and get you ready for Kim at 9:30am Liz 11am-7pm Diane 7pm-stay overnight

Thursday May 5
Diane will stay thru rehab (until noon)
Liz noon-7pm
Aide 7pm-overnight
Friday May 6
*Anna Salamone flies into Palm Beach around 8:30 pm
Aide will stay until you go to Kim's at 9:30am
Diane 11:30am-2pm
Liz 2pm-7pm
Aide 7pm-overnight
Saturday May 7
Aide will stay until 10am
Patricia 10am-7pm
Aide 7pm-overnight
Sunday May 8
Patricia 10am-8pm
Diane 8pm-overnight
Monday 5/9
Diane will stay until around 11am
Liz 11-7pm
Patricia 7pm-overnight

Tuesday May 10
Patricia will stay until you go to Kim's
Liz 11am-6pm
Diane 6pm-9pm
Patricia 9pm-overnight
Wed May 11
Liz 11am-6pm
Diane 6pm-9pm
Patricia 9pm-overnight
Thurs May 12
Patricia will get you to Kim 9:30am
Liz drives Diane to airport
Liz 11am-7pm
Patricia 7pm-overnight
Friday May 13
Patricia will take you to Kim at 9:30am
Liz 11am-7pm
Patricia 7pm-overnight
Saturday May 14
Carmen 8am-8pm
Patricia 8pm-overnight
Sunday 5/15
Carmen 8am-8pm
Patricia 8pm-overnight

Monday May 16 Liz 11-7pm Patricia 7pm-overnight	
Tuesday May 17 Patricia will take you to Kim's. Liz will meet you at Kim's at 9:30am Liz 9:30am-6pm *Diane here for dinner 6pm-9pm Carmen 9pm-overnight	
Wed. May 18 NO SPEECH THERAPY Carmen will take you to 　　Niele/Francis at 　　10am Liz 11am-7pm Carmen 7pm-overnight	Diane flies to 　　Philadelphia Diane 10am Phoner Daily Express Another phoner 12:30 pm UK version of 　　Associated Press
Thurs. May 19 Diane Flies to West Palm Beach	
Friday May 20 ***DISCHARGE***	

27

Came the Day

Came the long-awaited day of my departure from rehab, so many farewells to those who had steered my course these last three months. Saying good-bye to Kim was easy. She was away on holiday in Barcelona, we had already expressed our adieus. Niele promised a farewell kiss, which we somehow neglected in the rushed climax of departure, but I hope it was understood. Diane, Liz, Francis, and an eager intern delivered me to our rented condo whose intended winter season of basking in the sun, writing novels and swimming had been so rudely interrupted by my fall.

Francis had promised to put his eagle eyes to my safety. After he inspected for difficult snags—places where I might fall—and declared it safe, he prepared to depart. Was this all? Well-wishes, expressions of gratitude, papers signed, and I was home. A free man, honorably discharged.

Sunlight streamed through the window. No cacophony of caregivers. No early morning blood drawn from my veins. My mind drifted from books planned but interrupted, back to Gardens Court where we had made so many friends and acquaintances, a place where you were greeted by name each time you were met. Amazing to say. I basked in the sun and the silence, watching the dust motes dance. Fully restored? No, still confined to wheelchair, but all adieus from Gardens Court had cheered me to keep improving. I intended to.

My first visitor was a therapist who knew Francis and was of the same caliber. An imposing Latin American who spoke fluent English, his visit was compulsory, being part of the system following up with recent patients of rehab. He explained his vision to me: that my leg and hand continue to regain life.

Next to arrive was a succession of nurses whose main concern was with paperwork, half-a-dozen forms whose meaning craftily eluded. Beware of identity warblers, they seemed to be saying. Or walruses. Something like that, anyway. Having spelled it all out, they took their several leaves of us. What they left behind them was manna for the undiscerning eye. We wondered what in the world they had intended to convey.

Guess who came next? Why, Carmen of course, who had driven up to see what more she could do to set me free. She was as bright and prosperous as ever, still learning Russian and still versed in her catechistic conjunction, "Please expose your bottom, Mr. West, so we can make you clean for your wife." Now who can resist so tactful an offer.

There were no more visitors. No more soft options to misunderstand or to shrink from, clad in impish one-dimensional documentation from Mars.

But now a new obsession. Over and over—and ever after it sometimes seemed—the question was being raised of how I would travel home, north to Ithaca by air. Not an abstract casual question, but how would I respond to being shaken and shoved, bandied about and subjected to the whole experience of flying at several hundred miles an hour. I had served three years with the Royal Air Force and flown for thousands of miles, but I was 81 now, no spring chicken, and fresh out of rehab.

When flight day came and all the talk of wheels and lifting and chairs and methods of transport had fallen into a black hole, I rose to the occasion and sauntered up the ramp, step by step. Left. Right. Left. Right. Boarding the plane on my own feet, *sans* wheelchair. I amazed myself and wondered if I was real.

The same process applied when the plane touched down three hours later. Having slept through most of the journey, step by step, I disembarked. This, from a man who just months ago could not lift his right leg. Was I dreaming?

28

Rialto

Diane and I rode home from the airport, driven by our long-time friend Chris, an impressive and genial factotum who had news to share from the literary Rialto. It was good to be back among the temperate, winter-loving Ithacans, after all we had been through in the heat of the Florida winter. Diane and I had been away for seven months, had stories to tell friends, and to each other as well, having been apart so long.

Home at last, I had one gift to bestow on my wife. A radiant bouquet of a dozen stamens, rich purple in hue, to which she gave a silky thanks, mindful of the things we had just lived through. She was in tears. It was not over, not by a long shot, but we had survived thus far.

"Just think of the unpaid bills," she said, with wincing sobriety.

"I do." I, vocal for once. We paused and then burst out laughing as we contemplated the flowers as if they were the whole world.

29

Landscape

For Diane, the impasse had been as frantic as it's possible to be, with convalescent spouse on the one hand, and literary career on the other. This stroke, my second, had called for a pell-mell all hands on deck, no holds barred. Diane had dutifully completed book tour returning to snatch exhausted evenings with her ailing counterpart. It had not been a good time to be on Earth, for either of us.

The reviews of her book, however, had been sumptuous, full of national and international praise. *100 Names for Love* was a memoir of Diane's care-giving and my recovery from my first stroke, which had left me physically intact, but aphasiac; in its essence, I'd completely lost access to my lifelong treasured trove of words. Over the course of years, I'd relearned how to communicate—repairing the damage to the language centers of my brain.

The memoir's best review had run in *The New York Times*, with the reviewer stating this tale of our transcending this adversity had restored his faith in human nature, and the paper had included a splendid photograph of us both. We sank back, well satisfied, although the book's triumph had made a botch of our private lives.

During these long months of rehab, Diane had made the best of it. She arrived when she could, bringing her own dinner as our food habits (as always) were utterly incompatible; sometimes spending the night, to be gone by breakfast. Carmen, Liz, and Patricia had filled in the gaps for us, each in her own immaculate way. Carmen with Russian, Liz with tales of her husband's eccentricities, Patricia with her grasp of literature—including some samples of Samuel Beckett.

Finally home alone, our lives gratefully lapsed into almost forgotten silence. Diane wondered aloud which Florida flower was blooming in the subtropics now. The orchid with purple stamens? Perhaps. I exhausted my meager vocabulary—spoken that is—signaled Diane to wait, and so she did. The signal one of those things that promises feast but promotes famine instead.

30

220 Pounds

Liz had been left behind in Florida to pack up after delivering us to the airport. She was to follow us north in a few days, driving the freeway in easy spell from Palm Beach to Ithaca. She would be the last to leave, and was to receive the landlady's unwarranted wrath at the state we had left the place in (a few lamps that no longer worked required new bulbs). We flew and she drove, but she was happy to do so. Liz soon enough would re-encounter the hen-scratch of P.W. the sinister as I gave up on wielding a pen in my right hand—it was time to launch my left-handed literary career. Liz lives in Washington now, to be near her mother. I miss her more than either of us can say.

But in no time, it appeared, we fitted ourselves with new caregivers, one whom we liked at once. This was Melissa, a full-voiced beauty whose vocal repertoire included a tiny other voice designed to reassure children and insecure adults. Before she came to us, Melissa had worked in Kendall, a nursing home nearby, where she had cooked up a storm of indulgent dishes for the inhabitants of this prestigious institution for elders. It is she who continues to persuade my hand and arm to behave normally, having been trained in restorative work.

Further notes on our Melissa. Her face without its charming smile, I have never seen. She is full of tender regard for all things life-affirming whether at the hospital, supermarket, or grave. Into the bargain, she has a photographic mind, has as yet to fly on a plane, and her ballerina training has been converted into a trim step forward. She has a capacious gift for dusting crockery and other fine things. In short, she is a gem.

I soon met Mark, Ithaca's expert in rehabilitating legs and arms, highly educated and soon also to earn the sobriquet of compassionate slave driver as Mark now taught my body the rules of the road. Fitting successor to the fabulous Francis, Mark was the one who pronounced me fit to lift 220 pounds on the leg press machine. To my delight, Mark often broke into French while shepherding my wobbly career among the able-bodied.

Many times, Mark has saved me from falling headlong into rehabilitative contraptions I still have not the names for, orange cones on which you were allowed to tap your feet, or an over-sized rubber ball which you were to catch or kick. Such fun to be had.

Last recruit in my quiver was a speech therapist whose expertise persuades me back to full-voiced resonance after months of sibilant whispering. After several months of tongue-twisting exercises, I was judged competent to advance from monosyllabic rant to reciting prose, but never before the full regimen of warm-ups:

1. Stick tongue in and out _____ times.
2. Move tongue from side to side on outside of mouth _____ times.
3. Touch your nose with your tongue _____ times.
4. Lower your tongue toward your chin _____ times.
5. Make a circle with your tongue around the outside of your lips _____ times. Change direction and repeat _____ times.
6. Move your tongue along the upper and lower teeth _____ times.
7. Push tongue against cheek inside mouth alternating sides _____ times.
8. Elevate tongue behind upper teeth _____ times.

It was this speech therapist who reintroduced me to Scrabble, from which I had taken a long holiday. Whatever we came up with in our silent ponders, I was conscripted to pronounce. Each word clearly and with voice upraised. Occasionally she handed me over to her equally competent and personable sidekick, who has also been a pleasure to work with these past months. All my speech therapists have had the gift of patient listening without which there is no progress, I hereby declare them members nonpareil of my illustrious rehabilitation team, ever pleasant to a gimpy adult who has forgotten how to speak.

My new hand therapist was, in her drill-sergeant way, officious and high-handed, especially at first. Among her habits was slapping my strong hand when I used it to assist my lagging right and perpetually belaboring explanations of my treatment. She was a yoga practitioner too, but why must she obsess about it? She once removed the skin from my right arm in a friction treatment that did not work anyway.

But with so many humble practitioners around me, why complain? For all I know, she was proficient in her declared profession.

31

Labor Day, 2011

Labor Day, 2011. The day is aptly named for me. I wake at three in the morning to continue this treatise. Diane and I now retire together about 11 pm, and she rises at 7 am. We used to go to bed separately, she at a normal hour, I at 5 am to sleep 'til noon. Life has forced us together in so many ways, and this most recent joint venture into slumber is one of the best.

    I wake first, and pad out into the gloom, flashlight in hand. Barefoot, I locate the wheelchair parked nearby, then push the door open to clear my muddled way. I manage well enough on the feat of closing doors, but not so well in opening them up. It is not the easiest way to make an exit at six in the morning, but so long as it doesn't wake Diane up, it's not bad. I, of course, cannot get into my customary polo shirt unassisted, but have an old robe which opens at the front and I wear it unbuttoned. Then with laborious zeal I get to work, script still an imperfect scrawl with the left hand, praying one day soon to return to the paradise of the right.

Somewhere in Cortland (not far from here) the newly married Mark is sleeping the sleep of the just and *comme il faut*—he would appreciate my French. He has inhuman tact and energy—I cannot be easy to deal with, the 81 year old with speech impediment, blighted hand and weakened leg.

There have been triumphs, as well as disasters, such as my fallible response to walking the wobbly soft surface of Mark's practice mat. How many times has Mark caught me from falling as I stumbled my way through yet another therapy session, vainly clutching my cane and balancing so precariously on my two legs?

I can hear the rhythm of Mark's counting as we walked and walked and walked, on some occasions to the outside world, where I navigated through a landscape of clumps of unmowed grass designed by a madman, hearing only Mark's count of how much further to my left, then right, at some point to half-fall restrained only by his providential hands.

How well I remember this voice, his injunctions to excel accompanied by "Now repeat the sidestep." Or the relief I felt on being transferred to the recumbent bike whose steady beat soothed me—the oft-repeated command to kick an enormous ball did not. Neither did the so-called dynamic balance practice, standing still, eyes closed, commanded to turn my head to the right and then the left, which climaxed as often as not in disaster.

All in all, I perform reasonably well. I remind myself why I come here in the first place: To repair as best I may the damage I had inflicted on my body. A poor bet, but my last resort. Fail these demands and I would turn into a permanent wheelchair citizen.

I have prospered under the guidance of these two gentle souls, Francis and Mark, two men somehow easily pleased in their Teutonic, insistent way. I couldn't help liking the therapists for their commitment to it all. Time after time, they rehearse the same despotic dogma, convinced as the archbishops of the need to express their creed to the great unwashed. They may disagree on matters of style, preference, and good taste, but in basics the therapists were inseparable. This must be so, otherwise everything comes apart and the aspirant falls to feckless doom.

It isn't the same with literature and the arts where opinion and tone rule supreme, or just about. In the arts, there is room for deviation of opinion; the symbolists versus the realists, the purple prosists against the plain style. They are both wrong; they are both right. But not with rehabilitation, not according to Francis and Mark anyway, and other apostles of their type. Of course there is room for minor variations, but not much. There is no optional way to skin this cat. Feet narrowly spaced will cross and cause a fall sooner or later. As common sense reveals.

And that disappoints me in some way. Surely this absolutism breeds an ideal training ground for monomaniacs. But not so. If a man barely human—or a capricious juggler—the same exquisitely democratic rules apply. I am never disappointed with egalitarianism, and therefore I take my stand, while cursing the suffering the chair has inflicted on my private parts.

32

Trying to Tell a Story

Back in the golden years before illness hastened my retirement from teaching graduate students the whys and wherefores of European fiction, I was offered a job at the BBC for the supposedly mellow resonance of my voice. I turned the position down, but agreed to a series of talks about fiction, which later evolved into one of my first books. Eventually the CBC in Canada broadcasted *Critically Speaking*, a program which some people actually remember.

My voice at that time was standing me in good stead. I emigrated to the USA, to which I was drawn, where I spent a welcome career at Columbia University soon after leaving Oxford. My troubles began much later with a miniature stroke known as a transient ischemic attack, which somehow denatured my voice, for a short time reducing it to a mere murmur. Another stroke six years later reduced it to being a slight sylph of its proper self. And this most recent stroke had completed the damage.

Now, at the speech unit of Ithaca's hospital I became a regular visitor hailed as a model client. In therapy, I was introduced a microphone, placed it right in front of me several inches from my nose. And I began the long haul of recovering my old voice to replace the sibilant shrew I had become accustomed to. I was on the road again from a fate worse than the death I was getting ready for, no longer to be a simulacrum of myself, whispering to my friends.

After such a prolonged mute preamble, what joy to find another voice to air my woes. I was commanded to strive, full-voiced as I could, for sounds that could gladden only a speech therapist's heart. "Say *ba* into the mike. Then *ba ba,* repeatedly. Then *How Now, Brown Cow.*" I did as I was told, rising to crescendo with *Brrroown Cooow*, with a shade of my former gusto.

I tried again, and again. Bludgeoning my voice to produce the melismatic afterbirth—as I jokingly called it—of my former oratorical glory.

"In spite of falling away at the end," she judged, "not bad at all. Consider yourself repaired!"

I was overjoyed. This author of 50 books was alive at full volume again, ready to be tested anew. But not all was yet well.

She paused before commenting further, "Your response to the microphone test proves that your voice is capable of volume. What else is going on? You say that your nose fills with mucus and your eyes pour with tears the instant things go wrong in your throat."

I had to admit it.

I said the word "phlegm" and awaited her response, which wrote off phlegm as an excuse from God in a bad mood.

"What else?"

"That would not explain your reluctance to pronounce the last word when I ask you to read sentences. Always you drop the last word."

I did not know how to being to explain—I could not read the right margin of a page. Residue from my first stroke, my vision lopped off the ends of sentences, to my chagrin, and apparently to speech therapy's confusion. Although I was used to it.

I tried to say the word *different*, but could not. The ghost of Christmas stalks these highline passes, like a snowstorm in the heart and will carry on doing so forever. Once again, I could not speak.

Among other ceaselessly unfolding pleasures there is a new game requiring me to complete an innocuous sentence, resulting in my uttering quite a few blasphemous proposals. More to my taste was contemplating a six-sided cube emblazed with short phrases, which we combined to make nonsense or—rarely—brilliant ripostes or aperçus. The unpredictable quality of the prank appealed to me, but I cried out for more subtlety and more variety, unlikely as that might be.

    I have always looked forward to romps with words. For the moment, these are with a genial professional with a deadly sense of purpose—which was decidedly my return to a language of discourse beyond the figments that ran through my head anxious to get out. Pipe dreams have no more willing applicants than I.

33

Self-Similar

And so—as John Keats called them—the tall senators of the mighty woods, the trees, lost a touch of their glamour, falling into senescence once again, not harshly, but enough to irreduce themselves. I am a sucker for trees, especially ones that cry. Imagine such a structure with a broken heart.

- It has a fine structure at arbitrarily small scales.
- It is too irregular to be easily described in traditional Euclidean geometric language.
- It is self-similar (at least approximately or stochastically).
- It has a dimension which is greater than its topological dimension.

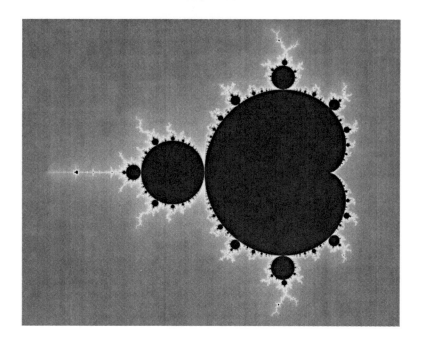

There, I've said it. The life story of a tree, a fellow fractal. A tree, anyway, is always a tree.

My tree reverie goes back in time to childhood when I climbed a tree and to celebrate the feat fell on my head and conked out. A history of falling, indeed. Later, much later in fact, I fell again and to all that this book narrates. After some hesitation, classic fumbles, and learning to write in a sinister hand, John Keats and I still have control of our trees and destiny. His a mighty woods; mine a little sapling, but a tree and a destiny nonetheless.

As I said, Keats and I rule the trees, and they are glad to accept domination. A tree is not a flower, but many have thought so and thus been deceived. Any more than a flower is a pound cake. It takes a lot of discontinuities to pontificate in this manner, but I shall persist, knowing how difficult it is to separate truth from lies. When the part already includes the whole, you wonder at the redundancy.

I can go on like this for hours right after my daily nap. Rambling, some might call it, but to me it is the soul of sanctity, helping me get from one day to the next. And if I doubt, I consult my memories of my mentors, Francis or Mark or Niele or Kim, the restorative preceptors who keep my mind on the straight and narrow.

For practical purposes—my balance is still precarious—I remained harnessed to my wheelchair. But I get about quite well. I must maintain dreams of promise or something similar, not pipe dreams but first-class reveries right out of the sketchbook of Benoit Mandelbrot. Could anything be more fractal than that?

Well, good night now. I wish you a pleasant slumber without too many mosquitos flying about. I have come far in your presence and will go much farther for emasculation. I should have said embrocation. I'm sorry.

34

Beyond Everything

Chain mailed, as from a distant century, he bestills my emotions like a Colossus, spear at the ready, dagger on his shield, his expression fierce, unwavering. He is a Crusader, born to fight a thousand years, except he is halved at the middle, having no trunk at all. He is Saracen, born only half a man, designed to fight my battles for me, whether in the Crusades or the War of the Roses. He alone survives the slaughter, brings home to me the enemy's skull. Why I require him to perform thus, year upon year is an open question. Perhaps an old man prefers others to do his fighting for him which is to say for the last fifty years. As now, when all the forces are ranged against me, some old and tremulous, some alert, god-fearing and young. Now I will do battle with the Almighty himself. Aphasia, apraxia, stroke, zeitgeist, and wanton hubris.

What is my suffering like? My strokes have given me something to obsess upon, and come to terms with perhaps never. Or, say, perhaps in the beyondness of everything. A poor thing, but mine own. Man is magnificent. No need to bite the bullet, no need to eat the gun.

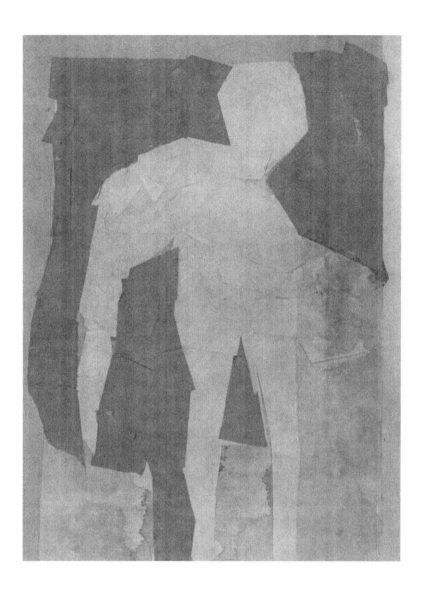

"A great writer."
—Hector Bianciotti, front page, *Le Monde*

"West is an extraterrestrial, and while he flies over he sometimes looks down on us poor word-birds pecking at our corn."
—William H. Gass

"One of the most consistently brilliant lyrical writers in America... [West is] possibly our finest living stylist in English."
—*The Chicago Tribune*

"West has been for several decades one of the most consistently brilliant writers in America. His aim seems to be the rendition of an American odyssey analogous to Joyce's union of mythic elements in which earth-mother, shaper-father and offspring, as well as the living and the dead, all achieve communion. The language is Paul West at his best.... shows perfect pitch."
—Frederick Busch, *Chicago Tribune*

"West, prolific novelist and critic, is a literary high-wire artist, performing awe-inspiring aerial feats with language while the rest of us gape up at him in dumb amazement."
—*The Boston Globe*

"Out on those risky ledges where language is continually fought for and renewed—that's where Paul West breathes the thin, necessary air."
—Sven Birkerts, *American Energies*

"A rich, often astonishing meditation upon how a particular human culture can represent a source of 'otherness'—imagination itself—that persists even in a world that other modes of thought and desire have made almost uninhabitable."
—Thomas R. Edwards, *The New York Times Book Review*

"His is one of the most original talents in American fiction."
—*The New York Times Book Review*

"Paul West's epic touches upon the most powerful human themes—the meaning of home, the desecration of war, the quest for a curative past out of spiritual exile."
—Bradford Morrow, *Trinity Fields*

"West's enormous pastiche of yarn-spinning, meditation and sheer wordplay is precisely the sort of work that can help us understand the ways in which we approach and avoid the realities of being human…. Paul West is a worthy custodian of a time-honored tradition."
—Alida Becker, *The Philadelphia Inquirer*

"West's astonishing new novel, which maps the lives of Indians in the American Southwest, reveals a Joycean genius in its exuberant play of language, and its epic and mythic resonances…. West's prose, dazzling in its fecundity, affirms the erotic nature of the literary act."
—*Publisher's Weekly*

"West is a master."
—*Washington Post Book World*

"Intoxicated by the novel's unparalleled capacity to connect life and ideas in an unholy mix, he likes fireworks in his fiction, the blow-torch of art that brings reality to the boiling point…. Thorough, passionate, opinionated—West never lets his judgments interfere with his considerable ability to evoke the texture and character of the work under review."
—*Washington Post Book World*

"A writer of distinction and originality."
—*The Los Angeles Times*

"West is an original and daring writer…he has never written anything so risky and triumphant."
—Richard Eder, *Los Angeles Time Book Review*

"No contemporary American prose writer can touch him for sustained rhapsodic invention—he creates a hyperbolic hymn to joy, a swashbuckling swirl of sentences. West stands as an authentic voice in the wilderness, a visionary who plugs the ghosts of history and morality into his textural dream machines."
—*Boston Phoenix*

"In his many works of fiction, memoir, and criticism, West proves himself to be a writer blessed with a cheerfully mordant wit, an acrobatic way with words, ebullient learnedness, and a deep if wry perception of the human condition. Each previous *Sheer Fiction* volume has offered pleasure, revelation, and provocation, and now, in West's fourth collection of biting literary essays, he again covers a remarkable breadth and complexity of terrain."
—*A.L.A. Booklist*

"West argues passionately for a literature that reveals brilliant minds at work shaping it, that incorporates the world we know today—quantum physics, computer technology…. [His] argument is likely to provoke much disagreement, especially from the academic community… Yet his argument needs to be heard. …*Sheer Fiction* demands the attention of any reader seriously interested in the purposes of fiction."
—*Wilson Library Bulletin*

"This kind of infectious enthusiasm is rare to the point of non-existence among modern critics. …Sheer pleasure."
—*Kirkus Reviews*

"The inimitable, brilliant Paul West never ceases to amaze. *Love's Mansion,* orchestrated with Proustian care, offers unforgettable episodes of familial dark and light, bittersweet recollections activated by empathy and sexual awareness. A revelatory book of extraordinary power."
—Walter Abish

"*The Tent of Orange Mist* is a bold, shocking book, filled with cynical brilliance and sensual power."
—*The Boston Review*

"Paul West is one of American literature's most serious and penetrating historical novelists. *The Tent of Orange Mist* is a gorgeous assertion of human life."
—*The San Francisco Chronicle*

"If there are no 'men of letters' any more, there are innumerable figures writing now…who move easily among the fictional, the confessional, the polemical, and the critical. If Paul West is not the most conspicuous of such a group, he is the most stylish and intelligent."
—*Journal of Modern Literature*

"A towering astonishing creation."
—Irving Malin, *Pynchon and Mason & Dixon*

"Paul West's book is transformative. West's immense narrative gift has transformed a traumatic historical event into art. He has re-imagined experience and made literature from it. His book will live."
—Hugh Nissenson, *The Song of the Earth*

"It takes a writer like Paul West to explore the deep psychic lacerations occasioned by [9.11]… Anyone who thinks he or she knows anything about that harrowing moment should read this novel; it will change their perceptions forever."
—David W. Madden, *Understanding Paul West*

""West's phenomenal command of language and the flux of consciousness, and his epic sense of the significance of 9.11 are staggering in their verve, astuteness, and resonance."
—Donna Seaman, *Booklist magazine*

"Not since Proust's *Albertine disparue* has a novel explored the subject of anguish and loss with such unflinching persistency and such annihilating force. This book will have you on tenterhooks and will break your heart."
—Mark Seinfelt, *Final Drafts*

"Paul West, among our more formidable literary intelligences, is not afraid to take risks. His ability to give original expression to complicated ideas about culture and personality is gargantuan. *The Place In Flowers Where Pollen Rests* presents a stunning, hyperbolic vision of men between cultures, between darkness and light, groping for authenticity."
—Dan Cryer, *Newsday*

"Extraordinary in its scope, inventiveness, and prose…. spectacular writing."
—Gail Pool, *Cleveland Plain Dealer*

"An exciting and evocative tale of love and treason."
—Andrew Ervin, *The Philadelphia Inquirer*

"While this biting, scatological tour de force will appeal mostly to West fans and more experimental poetry readers (many of whom are already West fans), it deserves a prominent place in poetry collections."
—Rochelle Ratner, *Library Journal*

"An exhilarating collection…. West's genuine excitement for this fiction is contagious and his own language is as splendid."
—*Review of Contemporary Fiction*

"[This novel] thrusts us into a rich domestic situation that reflects the complexities of our century like a prism. *Love's Mansion* is the late 20th century's contribution to the great, classical love novels of history."
—Elena Castedo

"[*The Tent of Orange Mist*] is both a terror and a joy to read."
—Kathryn Harrison

"The rest of us will despair of ever being able to write prose so immaculate as that of Paul West."
—Jonathan Yardley

"Most intriguing is the overarching narration told by Osiris, god of the Nile, who comments on this swarm of events with hilarious and humane authority. Profound and entertaining, *Cheops: A Cupboard for the Sun* is perhaps Paul West's greatest novel yet."
—J. M. Adams

"West, a writer of finesse, amplitude, and wit…describes his father in startlingly tactile detail as he recounts the wrenching war stories his father told him…. West's sensitivity to the vagaries of temperament is exquisite, his tenderness deeply moving. Writing of wars past in a time of war, West creates a portrait of his father that has all the richness of Rembrandt as it evokes the endless suffering wars precipitate."
—Donna Seaman, *Booklist*

"For beautiful sentences fed on brainpower, there is perhaps no other contemporary writer who can match him."
—Albert Mobilio, *Salon.com, Reader's Guide to Contemporary Authors*

CPSIA information can be obtained at www.ICGtesting.com
Printed in the USA
BVOW010535071212
307473BV00001B/1/P